Because I Said So

Life In The Mom Zone

Annie Oeth

SARTORIS
LITERARY
GROUP

A traditional publisher
with a non-traditional approach to publishing

SARTORIS LITERARY GROUP
P.O. Box 4185
Brandon, MS 39047
www.sartorisliterary.com

To my three Dear Sons and my Dear Daughter—you will always be my heart

CONTENTS

Part 3: Growing Up

Part 4: Home Sweet Home

Part 5: Matters of the Heart

FOREWORD

I've been blessed in my life, far more than I deserve. There are too many blessings to name, but four of them stand out.

Three sons plus one daughter add up to more pride, joy and challenge than I think I can stand some days. But blessings all come disguised as work. All four have been far more joy than challenge.

I have now been a mama for more years than I haven't been one. Those four blessings, three sons and a daughter, have defined—more than anything or anyone—who I am and what I believe. Everything I do is preceded by thoughts of them and how what I do affects them. They are my heart, an inseparable part of me.

At twenty-one, I graduated from Mississippi University for Women and married the next week, but the real education began about thirteen months later, when the first Dear Son came along.

I like to think that he and I grew up together. I was old enough to be considered an adult, but young enough not to realize how young I was at the time. Day by day, he grew up, and I did, too. The older I got, the less I knew.

His brothers and sister followed, bringing their own challenges and their own joy. After each was born, I'd wonder how in the world I had ever lived without that little boy or that little girl. Not being their mama was unimaginable.

No matter what else happens in my life, whatever blessings come my way, being a mama is the greatest title I could ever hope for. It's the worst-paying, hardest job ever, but the fringe benefits are worth it.

After being a mama for more than twenty-five years, I still melt whenever I hear an "I love you." When one of them hugs me, I don't want to let go.

I have friends and colleagues with young children and some who are expecting their first child. Bless their hearts, they don't have a clue what they are in for. Walking the floor at night with a baby turns into waiting up for a teenager only too quickly. They are in for more worry and trouble and happiness and pride and love than they could possibly imagine.

If I could only do one thing right in my life, it would be mothering. If you get that wrong, then getting everything else right wouldn't come anywhere close to compensating. When you become a mother, you realize that raising this child has just become the number one reason you are on the planet. Nothing else that goes on in your life, nothing that you dream about, nothing that you choose to do, large or small, is untouched by thoughts of this tiny person.

But none of us is perfect. I say the wrong thing sometimes. I lose my temper or my judgment is off, or I am just too tired to listen. But I try my best. I swing for the fences. Some days I strike out, but not every day. I'm thankful for those good days, and for most of us, they far outnumber the bad and the just plain stupid.

As a little girl, I remember declaring what I wanted to be when I grew up. Not what I wanted to do, but what I wanted to be, because they are not the same thing.

What you do is temporary and can change, just like you trade one job for another, or drift in and out of fitness classes or favorite places to do lunch. What you want to be is who you are, as much a part of you as your skin and your soul. You can stop what you do, but you can't stop being until you stop breathing.

I wanted to be a mommy, I said, most likely not five years past being a baby myself.

That was who I wanted to be, who I became and who I am. It is who I will continue being.

Being a mother goes far beyond giving birth. It is being there, being so good at caring and supporting and making sure the food's on the table and the lights are on that sometimes you get taken for granted at times. But you don't do all the things, the love, the care, the upbraiding and the pep talks, the boo-boo kissing and hugs, for a gold star. You do these things because doing them is part of who you are being.

And who you are, mothers, is beautiful.

Each of you is blessed, because each of you was given a precious mother and each of you has been given the gift of nurturing at least one human being into adulthood.

Years ago, when I had small children, I had a sweat shirt printed with the message, "God grant me the patience to endure my blessings."

My blessings are managing to endure me in all my well-meaning imperfection, and I am doing more than enduring motherhood. I am being a mother, and not simply doing. Even on bad days, I try never to forget that each of my blessings is a blessing, a gift, and should be treated as such.

It is my hope that you treasure as well as endure all your blessings and that these thoughts bring a smile not only to your face but to your heart.

Be blessed.

--Annie Oeth

Part 1

Celebrations
and
Other Causes for Alarm

THE TRUTH ABOUT SANTA CLAUS

Nothing strikes fear in a mama's heart like the idea that her babies might not believe in Santa Claus anymore.

Not believe in Santa Claus? Why, they might as well not believe in the tooth fairy.

I know I had my doubts at times.

When I was a little girl, I questioned how Santa could be at the Sears & Roebuck in West Point the same night that my friends saw him at Leigh Mall in Columbus. He has decoys, I was told. Doppel-gangers. Santa just can't see everyone everywhere so he has doubles. "Santa's helpers."

If I'd been thinking, I'd have questioned why, if he needed help with being everywhere for everyone before December 24, he didn't need help getting toys under all those trees on Christmas Eve.

But I was blinded by childhood greed. Those who asked too many questions about Santa Claus would get coal in their stockings. Or switches and ashes. Asking questions, it seems, was not quite as awful as being on the full-blown naughty list, but it was within spitting distance to it. It was as if, when he was making his list and checking it twice, Santa would pause, and think a little bit about your incessant questions, and then decide, out of the hot chocolatey goodness of his heart, not to condemn you to the list of bad kids. But you were super close to being there, you and your questions—so watch it.

I also thought it was quite a coincidence that Santa Claus' elves used the same kind of wrapping paper that my mama did. Hmmmm.

But whenever I'd ask questions, I would get the answer that those who believed got better stuff under the tree. My mama took great pleasure in having her only child believe for the longest period of time possible. Eventually, I just quit my questioning. For all she knew, I was in my late 30s, a mother of four, and a believer in Santa Claus.

And of course, my own children had questions about Ol' St. Nick.

For the oldest boy, the questions were quite loud. His class at South Side Elementary in West Point had taken a trip to McDonald's for breakfast with Santa. He was halfway through the second grade. No longer a trusting little first-grader, oldest boy was like a little Geraldo trying to bust open Al Capone's safe.

Questions followed questions that December, but when he saw Santa's Helper that day, he stopped with the questions.

You see, his teacher had asked a high school student, no doubt bribing him with a sausage biscuit, to come over to McDonald's dressed as Santa Claus. Getting out of class, plus getting a sausage biscuit, and getting to drive there? That's the trifecta for a high school student.

So oldest boy, having hung around the newsroom way too much because of his mama's profession, was watching a 120-pound young man stuff pillows in a Santa suit to keep the britches up and make an appropriate Santa gut.

It was all he could take. Santa Claus does not stuff his gut with anything other than sugar cookies. He does not have acne. And he arrives where he is going in a reindeer-powered sleigh, not a green and white Chevy pick-up.

"Santa's not real!" he yelled in his best outside voice. Then, trying to rally his classmates into a chant, he followed with, "Santa's a fake, Santa's a fake."

I knew this because I was there, chaperoning the outing, so I got the looks from the other mothers and the teather. Looks that said, "For God's sake, what is wrong with you? Get your kid to hush NOW."

Because if he didn't hush, there would be more kids asking questions. Pretty soon, we'd have a whole town full of nonbelievers.

"Honey," I whispered, trying to calm him down, "Stop. You're messing this up for the others."

"But he's not real," he said.

And I couldn't insult his intelligence. "This one's not real," I said, sounding a whole lot like his grandma. "But Santa himself is real."

And just like I stopped asking my questions years earlier, he stopped asking his, figuring either I wouldn't tell him the truth about Santa Claus or that—and read this in a Jack Nicholson voice—he couldn't handle the truth.

The next two dear sons didn't try to incite a riot with their conclusions about Santa Claus, but the youngest, my Dear Daughter, having all but made up her mind about the matter, decided to tell a few kids at the local Christmas parade that Santa might not be real and that parents are big, fat liars. OK, she didn't say the big, fat liar part, but that could be inferred by the tone in her voice.

A couple of parents told me to keep her on a short leash, cast a few aspersions on my parenting, and wished me a merry Christmas. I began to wish that I had a shot of peppermint schnapps in my hot chocolate. Don't judge.

Not long after that, she skipped into the kitchen while I was cooking dinner, scuffling along in her pink cowboy boots.

"Tell me the truth," she said, looking up at me with her big brown eyes, being as serious as she could be. "Is Santa real?"

And that is the corner we mamas paint ourselves into. We don't want to outright lie to our children, and we don't want to insult their intelligence either.

So we hope the question doesn't come, or dodge it, or bribe the kiddos with promises of a larger Christmas haul if only they don't ask too many questions.

I babbled along about the real Santa being the spirit of giving and the spirit of Christmas, and I may have sung a few bars of that song about Christmas shoes.

She was having none of it.

"Is Santa real?" she persisted.

"OK," I said, "You are old enough to know the truth. Santa, is real. He is as real as I am."

She stared at me silently for a while, looking my face over for tells like a poker player, but my gaze was steady.

Then her eyes opened wider.

"Ohhhhh," she said, knowingly. "Thanks, Mom.''

MOTHER'S DAY 2.0

There are some days that are just awful.

They are dreaded every year. There's no use in avoiding them because there is no way to do that and remain above ground.

You just have to get past them.

Father's Day is one of those days. After Baby Daddy and my own sweet daddy passed on in the same year, we began to hate Father's Day.

We didn't have anything to celebrate or anyone to do things for on a day for fathers. It became a day for skipping church because I didn't want my children to be the only ones making a Father's Day card for their mama. For a while, we avoided restaurants because there would be all these daddies and kids there. But we do like to eat, so we either fired up the grill or we just ate out anyway.

Every few years someone gets in trouble for talking about daddies and single mothers. Who knows? Maybe it will be me this year. I have been a single mama for about eight years now, and while I can bring home the bacon and fry it up in a pan, and I can cut the grass and hand out come-to-Jesus talks to the kids, I can't be a daddy.

Once the Dear Daughter had a father-daughter dance to go to and she went with me, since the thought of coming along with me was less horrifying than showing up with one of her brothers. She was the only girl there without her daddy, and no amount of electric sliding could turn me into one.

We've learned over the years to just avoid events with the word "father" in them.

But I would secretly celebrate Father's Day. Celebrate is not exactly the right word for the first time or two. More like it was a time I would do something nice for myself as a "happy" for the times I have to do dad-like things. But why do something nice for myself when I have a houseful of kids to do something nice for, too?

So instead of Father's Day, we now celebrate what the second Dear Son has dubbed Mother's Day 2.0.

Mother's Day 2.0 is celebrated much the way Mother's Day 1.0 is, by me taking the crew out to eat and picking up the tab, but that's OK. When you're a mama, paying the check is a small price to pay for having a table ringed by your sweet babies. If it is the sweet babies and me eating Japanese food, even better.

We had to redefine the day as a time to celebrate—yes, celebrate!—everything we've been through. We celebrate our family as it is, how close we are and how much fun we have together. We usually eat way too much and continue the celebration into everyone lapsing into a coma from overeating.

The name of our family holiday gives me pause to think, as there are a lot of single parents out there doing double duty. There should be some Father's

Day 1.0s in May for those dads who have to take their daughters shopping for bras. They can't feel any more comfortable than I did when I had to take my youngest Dear Son shopping for a jock strap.

Actually, I believe the youngest Dear Son was the most uncomfortable of all on that shopping trip. I am pretty sure that afternoon and the father-daughter dance will land him and his sister in counseling one day.

I can't truly be a daddy to my kids, any more than the men I know who play Mr. Mom can pull off going to a mother-daughter tea without horrifying their girls right into the counseling office next to the one my children will one day be in.

While what I was blessed to have grown up with—a mama and daddy who were hopelessly square, loved each other and were so predictable you could set a clock by them—is the ideal, not everyone has that.

And, by the way, it took years and years for me to wise up to how precious having a mother and father who love each other is. I had it really good and went around for decades taking it for granted. Married parents, if you can only give your children one thing, give them a fantastic marriage—yours! Never skip date night for your children. They will thank you later.

Go ahead and hate me, feminists. It's the truth. A child with two parents in the same house who love each other is better off. Why? Because there are two people in that house getting things done, loving on scrapes and tucking kids in with bedtime stories.

That is not saying that a single mother or a single father can't get the job done, but it is an easier life when you can do the parenting thing tag-team style. I can do my best, but at the end of the day, I can't be both a fully engaged mom and a fully engaged dad. There just aren't enough hours in the day or coffee in the pot for me to pull that one off.

And then there's the whole "I don't have a Y chromosome" thing. I can give it my all, but I can't be in two places at one time, and I can't teach someone to shave his face or tie a half windsor knot with any authority.

I focus on doing my own personal best because if it's my best, then what else have I got to give? And while I may be a single mom, it's not like I am truly in it alone. I've got four others in this family, and we're pretty tight.

We eat sushi together every Mother's Day 2.0.

FIREWORKS

This is a tale of maternal love, patriotism and betrayal about 14 years in the making, not counting the years America has been in existence.

Independence Day is one of our family's favorite holidays. How many other holidays can you grill out and blow things up to show your love of country? Sometimes the grilling and blowing up can happen at just about the same time, such as when I couldn't get the starter to work on the grill and took a match to the propane. My bangs needed a trim anyhow.

But for us, Independence Day is part holiday, part birthday-palooza. Two of my four children were born near the Fourth of July, and one year, the oldest son wanted to have a birthday party. Just a couple of friends. Just a little pizza and ice cream cake. Just shooting off a few firecrackers.

This all sounded reasonable to me.

So after a dinner of pizza and ice cream cake, the five of us, birthday boy, his younger brother who was about twelve at the time, and birthday boy's two buddies, set out for what I hoped were unincorporated parts of Madison County. Shooting fireworks is illegal in the city, but you can blow things up to your heart's content outside the city limits. Just a carload of middle school boys, a lighter and a box of bottle rockets and other as- sorted incendiaries.

What possibly could go wrong?

At first, nothing. We hit The Breakers, a neighborhood that I thought was outside the city limits. At least, I hoped it was. I try to be law- abiding.

We went to the soccer field there, my thought being that it was away from enough people so no one would be annoyed and was nowhere near a rooftop so no one's house would be burned down. And I would come back in the morning light to pick up any fireworks litter. I'm a natural worrier, so things like this occur to me.

Middle school boys, though, don't have an ounce of worry among them. None. They don't even have enough change among them to buy an ounce of worry.

On this night, they were cackling over the launch of bottle rocket after bottle rocket. The testosterone was heavy that night.

Then the brand new 14-year-old got one of the Roman candles out, as fate would have it, as a police cruiser was driving by. I honestly do not remember which city's finest this was, as it all happened so fast. Plus it was dark and I was busy being horrified by the events as they were unfolding.

My oldest child lost his mind that night and aimed his Roman candle at the police cruiser. He grew up into a bright young man, but I am betting Einstein at 14 would have aimed a Roman candle at a police cruiser. Fourteen-year-old boys' minds work that way.

The blue lights came on, and here is the good part. Two boys I carried for a combined year and a half, plus their friends, ran. Fast.

I was standing there with all the evidence in my hands, my mouth hanging open. I stammered an explanation and a heartfelt apology to the officers. Indeed, I was deeply regretting the whole night.

The four boys walked back up once the officers called for them, and, staring at their feet, said they were sorry. They got scolded for leaving the scene and their mama and for shooting fireworks at law officers.

No one was ticketed. I think the officers figured that having to hold a 14-year-old's birthday sleepover was punishment enough for me.

We all climbed back into my car, a little Saturn. It was close quarters, as the car had enough belts for five but not enough space. We drove back home, me being angry enough not to say much because anything that would have come out of my mouth would probably have been something14-year-old ears didn't need to hear, and the boys all afraid to say anything.

One word, I think they knew, might make me erupt like so many Roman candles.

SOMETHING SKANKY THIS WAY COMES

It's the skank-skankiest time of the year.

Of course, it's Halloween.

"It's the best holiday ever," I overheard the oldest, a college student at the time, say. "Every girl wears a miniskirt, fishnets and high heels."

It does a mama's heart good to know her son has high standards. But, alas, he is right. Halloween has become skankified.

When I was a little girl, adults didn't wear costumes, and kids' costumes, in West Point, Mississippi, were limited to whatever was at the Gibson's. That was a small-town Southern precursor to Walmart, a place that sold the basics, along with Mexican jumping beans and rabbit's foot keychains at the check-out counter.

Gibson's had a wide selection of get-ups. The choices were soldier, Frankenstein, Cinderella, witch, clown and ghost. Clown was the creepiest.

Each costume bag had a plastic smock that tied in the back and a mask held together with a rubber band. No kid made it through the night without the rubber band breaking.

None of these costumes were skanky. Or for adults. If you were past ten, they probably didn't have your size.

But today, the costumes are pricier, better made and quite a bit more creative, yet they are sexed up once you get to age twelve or so. The girls' costumes have sweet little princesses pictured on the labels for girls in elementary school. After that, it jumps to pre-teen skank and progresses to full-grown.

The stores have witches, clowns, soldiers. But they are not merely flying-around-on-a-broom witches or enlisted soldiers. They are "sexy witch" and "Sgt. Skank." They could double as a career investment if your profession happens to be the world's oldest.

There are those who say Halloween is an evil holiday. They hold harvest festivals without costumes, or if they want to be edgy, they might offer face painting. My family has never taken that viewpoint. My mama, a woman who read the Bible every morning, liked her Good Book the way she drank her coffee, strong and sweet. She'd dress me up as a little witch each October 31. It was all about the getting of candy.

It's still about the candy, and a pox on those who hand out apples and raisins. Those are for the other 364 days of the year. But it is also about people dressing to be naughty these days.

Part of my job as a mama during the Halloween season is to be the skank police. One year, my Dear Daughter wore a little girl's witch robe, mind you, with a slit up the side that went to hip level. I was the meanest mother in the world for making my Dear Daughter wear sweatpants underneath.

That is nothing new, though. I hold the Meanest Mother in the World title. I got it for putting the nix on the carrying of a fake bloody axe, and also for saying no to a mask that pumped fake blood. Those were wanted by my Dear Sons, who wanted to be horrifying just as much, apparently, as some girls want to be naughty nurses and bad girl pirates.

Market forces do make much of the world function, so either companies want skankiness out there, or there is a demand for it, because I don't care how sexy the costume is, no company is going to put it on store shelves unless it will sell to someone.

I haven't had the nerve to veer away from my Halloween basic, a turtleneck dotted with little Jack-O'-lanterns and black cats, to become a German beer wench to answer the door or take my children trick-or-treating, and this is from me, a woman who has taken great joy in embarrassing her offspring in other less skanky ways.

I am thinking one Halloween like that, and my children would land in counseling, which probably costs more than a skanky costume.

EASTER EGGS

I am convinced that Ayn Rand invented Easter egg hunts. There are few things so no-holds-barred bare-knuckles free market capitalist as a good old Easter egg hunt.

I got mine. You didn't get yours?

Survival of the fastest egg picker-uppers.

The Oeth kids are no good at group egg hunts. They're fine at the ones at home that I have livened up by putting money in some of the eggs, and their little hearts were happy at church egg hunts that were policed by moms and church staff. Each kid was to come in with a dozen eggs to be hidden, and no one was to leave with 13 in their basket at the end. If church egg hunts were an economic model, it might be Keynesian—no ebbs and flows, no crashes or bubbles, but all attempts to control were made repeatedly.

Public egg hunts are another matter. They are over in a matter of minutes, usually with a few kids having eggs galore, and the rest wondering what the hell just happened.

I work as an editor, or at least, that's what I tell the Boss Man. One fine spring day, I assigned a photographer to take photos at an egg hunt. I was thinking there'd be at least one magical photo of a child picking up a perfect pastel egg and laying it lovingly into her basket of plastic Easter grass.

Oh, no.

The photographer was stunned by the shock and awe of a stampede of little egg snatchers, half of them hopped up on jelly bean sugar, tearing after a field full of hen fruit. Before he could focus, it was over. There was no, "Pardon me, ma'am, but could I take your child's picture? And what is his name?"

And that is not even taking into account the parents who get involved. I assigned an egg hunt photo another Easter season, and the problem that year was getting a photo without the rumps of parents showing in the photos. Yes, you read that right.

That year, at the Mississippi Agriculture and Forestry Museum's egg hunt, there were quite a few parents who were going to make sure their little darlings had something in their baskets, and they weren't afraid to bend over and scoop up eggs themselves to make it happen. The irony … parents grabbing eggs so their children could enjoy an egg hunt. What's next? Let me eat that Cadbury Egg for you so you can enjoy Easter festivities without that sugar rush, calories or risk of cavities?

The trading floor at the New York Stock Exchange couldn't be any wilder than an egg hunt. I don't care if you are in a city of a million or a small town, egg hunts are a wild affair. Screaming, elbows flying, egg stealing … none of it would surprise me.

Churches only have them to give their members' children happy Easter memories. Although church egg hunts have given my Dear Daughter pause to ponder.

"Mama," she asked one day, "What do eggs and rabbits have to do with Jesus rising from the dead?"

I remember asking the same question myself as a girl, at least in my mind. Asking questions out loud about religion didn't go over so well for me back then. That was true of the time I asked what a harlot was after the preacher talked about one in his sermon. It was a "hit the brakes"'moment when I said, "Mama, what's a harlot?''

You'd at least think I would have gotten points for listening to the preacher in church, but no.

If "harlot'' would raise the ire of my parents, think what asking about the institutions of the Easter Bunny and Jesus would do. It wouldn't have been pretty.

But, being the child of someone who tells the Boss Man she's an editor, the Dear Daughter asks questions. Lots of them. To all kinds of people, including the preacher when he visited her Sunday school class.

Not wanting to be the one to anger any parents by making their sweet babies doubt the veracity of the Easter Bunny tale, the preacher switched gears in class but told her later what we all should have suspected. That egg hunts were pagan rituals kept alive when pagans became Christians.

Pagan roots in egg hunting shouldn't surprise anyone. Why else would they bring out the heathen in us all?

BE THANKFUL

Living a joyful life is nearly impossible without being thankful, but that is easier said than done.

When all is well—when there is enough money at the end of the month, when your home is off the pages of *Southern Living*, when you have an adoring spouse and children who never misbehave, say "yes, ma'am and yes, sir" and always are at the top of the honor roll, when you can do no wrong at the office and could pass for thirty when you're pushing fifty—then I could imagine being thankful would be easy.

I say "imagine" because I've never lived in that world I just described. I think the sign on that county line might be "Dreamworld—Population 0."

The rest of us? We live in the next county, where dollars have to be stretched, houses have long repair lists that seem to grow by the day. It's the place where your significant other is jumping up and down on your last nerve and your children are inventing new ways to be bad. It's the land of office disasters and passing for fifty when you're thirty.

"Real Life County—Population: Everybody."

There may be some folks whose life may look on the outside like they live in "Dreamworld," but the woman who looks like she has it all together doesn't. Maybe she is desperately lonely or has a marriage that is falling apart, only you don't see it. The family with the perfect home may be struggling to pay that house note each month and falling deeper into debt. The golden child at the office may be longing for the career path she didn't pursue. She may be great at a job that's not her passion and doesn't bring her happiness.

I never knew my grandmother, but my daddy used to repeat one of her sayings. "If problems were laundry, and everyone took theirs and hung them out on the line for everyone to see, I think we'd take ours back in." I used to imagine her collecting her problems, taking the clothespins off one by one and hauling them in like sheets in her laundry basket, taking ownership of them and happy not to have anyone else's troubles.

Maybe that is where we start. We take our problems and give thanks for them. They're our problems, after all. I've told my crew, when we've faced problems, that one day we would look back and laugh about this. And we have.

If things turned out "Dreamworld" perfect, where would the good stories come from? When you think about it, "Dreamworld" would be pretty boring. As Yogi Berra once said, if life was perfect, it wouldn't be.

So be thankful for challenges—that's often what problems really are—because they make us into better, stronger people. Maybe economic challenges encourage you to reevaluate your life, pursue a new career or scale back to living more simply with fewer headaches.

Be thankful for the little things that get on your nerves, for they can often be unintentional gifts from those you love dearly.

The whiskers in the sink my sons used to leave? I miss those now that they've grown up and moved off for their careers.

Socks on the living room floor? They came from a precious prayed-for child of mine, so I can grumble about the socks or be thankful for the boy.

Paints, brushes, pencils and paper scattered around the dining room? They're there because my artsy daughter is working on another project. She, and her creativity, are worthy of thanks, not complaints.

What about dirty dishes? Instead of arguing about who has to wash them, be thankful your dishes are dirty. Dirty dishes mean that you had a good meal, with leftovers in the refrigerator. Be grateful for those, too—leftovers mean you have more than enough.

A house that needs repairs? Be thankful you have a house.

A houseful of your children and their friends? Be thankful for the noise, because more than likely it is a joyful noise, and because it says your children think of your home as the kind of place they and their friends want to spend time.

A yard to mow? You have land, and a reeason for thanks. Few things give the sense of "before-and-after" accomplishment that mowing a yard does. I remind my children of this often.

Be thankful for hard work. It builds character and gives purpose. It's also the disguise that opportunity wears.

Lots to do both at home and at work or in your volunteer efforts in your community? That means you most likely have a dear family and friends, and are trusted by coworkers and have a part in helping others. Give thanks.

You're reading this, so someone must have cared enough to teach you how to read. Maybe you had loved ones who reinforced those lessons by tucking you in with stories of fairytale romance and adventure. Be thankful.

Be thankful for the miracle of life—the breath in your lungs and the beat of your heart, arms that can be strong as well as tender. You are part of that miracle, so give thanks.

To live with joy is to realize that each of us has been blessed more than we deserve, that our problems are smaller than we think and that all life's moments are to be embraced just like our children, as they are.

CHRISTMAS LIGHTS

I am an adult when it comes to Christmas lights. Let me explain.

Christmases ago, I rode in the back seat of my parents' Riviera as we drove around looking at Christmas lights. In West Point, in the early 1970s, there weren't that many spectacular light displays, so we'd ride for a while in a cold car before seeing something worth an "oh" and an "ahh." Being the antsy child I was, having to sit shivering in the back seat while the grown-ups talked and giggled was not always my idea of a fun evening.

Year by year, I grew into a hard-headed teenage girl, and if my parents went looking at Christmas lights, they most likely left me and my attitude at home. I didn't notice.

Christmases came and went. I matured a little more with each of them, becoming more like my father and mother, who could appreciate the quiet and peace of a Christmas drive, and less like a child who complained about being bored.

My mother never lost her love of looking at colored lights against an inky black winter sky, but making the drives became increasingly difficult each year.

In December 2003, she, my father and I, along with a couple of the Oeth kids, piled in my little five-seater Saturn and hit the drive-through for coffee and kids' meals before looking for the best lights Crossgates had to offer.

Mom was in a nursing home then, but we'd spring her out whenever she felt like an adventure. She had the best time that night—lights, fast food and her family around her.

It was her last Christmas season with us.

My father still liked to keep the tradition of looking at the Christmas lights, even without his wife of forty-four years, so he and I would bundle up the younger kids and hit the road to Canton. Few things can impress both septuagenarians and preschoolers, but Canton's square with its thousands of lights is one of them.

We went there together last in 2005. It was his last Christmas this side of Heaven.

The next Christmas, the night of Dec. 25, I got in the car alone and drove to Canton, circled the square and rode back home in silence. I'd have given anything to be back in that baby blue Riviera.

The kids and I go look at lights together now, and each year we do that is a treasure for me. Like pancakes before church on Sunday and Charlie Brown Christmas trees, it's a family tradition that I am grown enough to appreciate.

—Reprinted from The Clarion-Ledger

Part 2

A Mississippi Mama

NEW MAMAS

I remember the horror well.

It was deer-in-the-headlights terror. The head-lights, I was sure, were on the front end of a Mack truck.

I was about seven months pregnant with my oldest son. I was twenty-two at the time, married, a college graduate, a working journalist, and terrified.

"Well," I said to myself. "There is no getting out of this now."

My fear, at the time, was childbirth. Baby Daddy and I were enrolled in childbirth classes. In the meeting room of the hometown hospital, we'd talk about episiotomies, being cut from you don't want to know where to "Oh, God, no," and I would want to pass out. The day we took a field trip to the birthing room, I did. I think it was seeing the stirrups that did it.

And that is just like a rookie mama. First-timers are afraid of childbirth. Veteran mamas know birthing a baby is the easy part.

Yes, the labor, screaming, hollering, thanking Jesus for epidurals, a caesarian section. Totally the easy part.

My fear should have been not about physical pain. I should have been terrified about having to bring our baby home.

And when the time came, I was.

Being an only child and one of the youngest of the cousins in our family, I had no idea what to do with a baby. I had zero maternal instinct.

Everything in my system wanted to run in reverse the second a friend's child would need a diaper changed. Small children usually cried around me. The few times I babysat, it was for children about five or six years of age, and they were low maintenance. Make them a snack and give them a coloring book and some crayons and they were happy campers.

Crayons don't work with newborns.

Our boy had a rough start, so he was in the neonatal ICU for a while. His cardiologist told me on a Friday that I'd get to take him home the next day. I immediately thought that this was close to malpractice. Seriously, how could medical professionals trust me with a child? I mean, what were they thinking?

Just putting the car seat in my Honda was awful, and that was before I put the baby in. We somehow got home, and there were well-wishers. Friends and family came over, and the preacher's wife brought a pound cake. And then they left. Again, did these people not realize that Baby Daddy and I were morons with no child-rearing skills whatsoever?

Number one son was happy for a while, sleeping like the baby he was.

But babies also get hungry.

Breast-feeding zealots, chill out—I had to make him a bottle. The medical explanations and justifications of this would just kill the flow of this crazy story, so just know that I tried, and breastfeeding my oldest was just one more way I was overwhelmed in brand-new mama-hood.

So I was attempting to make a bottle. I had this neat Playtex bottle set that I could not figure out. The fact that I waited until I had a newborn screaming for dinner didn't help matters, but let's be honest: I was bumfuzzled on a good day.

I got the little plastic baggie liner inside the plastic cylinder, and I got the rest of the bottle parts together, sort of, but apparently I missed a step, because, when I tipped the bottle to feed this sweet little screaming miracle, he got a formula bath.

Again, I wondered, what the heck were these people thinking, leaving me to care for a newborn?

So, then, it was time for a bath. I sent Baby Daddy to go look for the Better Homes and Gardens Baby Book because it had pictures. I figured, if I could make my child's first bath look like the pictures in the book, then maybe he would survive the experience.

And although by now, this child of mine was turning red from hollering at us all, the bath went better than the first bottle at home. I figured out what I did wrong with the first bottle, and my child stopped cussing me out in baby language and finally got the newborn equivalent of a Big Mac.

He was sleeping again. And I could exhale for a little while.

And as terrifying as that first experience was, there was more to come. There were trips to the emergency room, stitches, a broken arm, a whole bunch of first days of school, learning to drive, graduations, moving into a college dorm, looking for a job, the first day at work and moving into his own place, several states away.

It all was scary for me, every second of it. But it was also a joy.

That baby's now older than I was when I doused him with Similac that first day home. Amazingly, I didn't kill him that day. I was more than a little worried I might. But he grew up into a man over the next twenty-five years.

There's more than a little truth to the old saying that God looks after fools and little children. He's managed to look over this fool and her little child for quite a while.

THE MOM ZONE

Back a year or more ago, one of my coworkers was getting a blog set up for me. I was going to write about mamas and families and things to do and whatever else stirred my imagination.

"What do you want to call it?" she asked on her way out of my office and over to hers.

"The Mom Zone," I said.

I wish I could say it was a carefully crafted name, studied with market demographics and audience share in mind. It wasn't. Like so many words do, I just opened my mouth and out they fell.

The Mom Zone it was.

From there, about five days out of seven, I am posting about life and crazy things and kids, celebrity baby names, recipes (and if you are what you eat, then I am cheap, fast and easy!) and whatever else enters my mind. It is amazing to me that the Boss Man pays me to do this stuff.

I truly have an enviable position. In my annual performance evaluation, I am told that I've been on Facebook a lot, and that's treated like a good thing. I give things away in contests. Books show up on my desk like clockwork every time the mail runs, and food companies send me their wares in hopes I will blog about it for *The Clarion-Ledger*. So far, I have gotten three boxes of frozen coconut water bars that I shared with the newsroom and a bottle of orange extract. Jealous?

The Mom Zone is a random place, perhaps in need of Attention Deficit Disorder medication, but if The Mom Zone blogosphere is like that, it's only because the real Mom Zone is like that, only moreso.

I spotted a meme that I more than likely shared on my Facebook page. It said thinking like a woman was like having 2,239 windows open on your computer. At the same time.

Being in The Mom Zone is like that, although I think the number of windows we have open is closer to 4,598.

Think about it. You've already got things to think about for just being yourself. There's the job and how you feel and what you're wearing, the music you like, your friends, the movie you want to see this weekend.

Then you enter The Mom Zone.

You're not just thinking about yourself anymore. Once the test stick turns positive, you are done thinking only about yourself. You will never think about only yourself ever again.

In The Mom Zone, you're thinking about whether your daughter remembered her lunch money. You're thinking about your son's test in science, do they have clean blue jeans, what's for dinner, your hubster, or in my case, my sweet gentleman friend. There's also the soccer game tonight, the parent-teacher conference, date night and did I pick up the dry cleaning.

There are these thoughts and more. Thoughts that might ordinarily been thoughts about you and your career drift into The Mom Zone. New duties at work? How will that affect my ability to leave the office in time to pick up children and get dinner on the table? Friends want to go out or go for a run or form a book club? What is the family going to say?

Tax refund or a raise at the office? Whose college fund will that be going to?

See what I mean?

Moms not only think a lot of thoughts about getting things done for all the people, small and large, in their lives, they do something about it. They layer tasks.

Remember the commercial from our childhood about the woman turning in for the night who whispers the secret, "I'm cleaning my oven?" Spraying the inside of the stove with oven cleaner before bed is a novice move.

In The Mom Zone, we paint our nails before cranking the car, so we can let them dry while whizzing down the interstate on the morning commute. While doing this, we also have a book on

CD in the stereo. There's dinner in the Crock Pot cooking while all this is going on. And we remembered to return our library books on the way out, and turned the self-cleaning oven on. Would that we had a self-cleaning house and a self-mowing lawn.

The Mom Zone is a place where we're all going about ninety miles per hour in fifteen directions mentally (on the interstate, that's a no-no) but for very good reasons.

It's for those we love. We want their lives to be good, and we're willing to do a daily juggling act to make that happen.

The Mom Zone also needs to be about moms doing a few things for themselves. It's the old adage about putting the plane's oxygen mask on yourself before you put it on your child. Really, if those oxygen masks fall often, I would switch airlines.

You have to take care of yourself first before you can care for those children and that man in your life. Otherwise, they all get a frazzled mess. And moms, the people who care for others so well, can be the worst at caring for themselves.

In The Mom Zone blogosphere, moms can relax a little, share advice, have a laugh, find something to make for dinner tonight and maybe find out how to enter a contest to win a trip to the spa.

In the real Mom Zone, where I live instead of where I blog, it's a busy place but one I try to carve a little "me'' time out of, if only to be the best mom, friend, coworker, significant other and me I can be.

EMBARRASS YOUR CHILDREN

Here is a simple, declarative sentence that you can use to direct your comings and goings. Ready?

Here it is: If you are not embarrassing your children at least a few times a month, you are not living life to the fullest.

This may sound like advocating a reckless and raucous lifestyle, but it is not. Embarrassing your children can be as simple as just showing up, if you happen to have a teen and a tween in the house.

Embarrassing older children takes a little more effort. Organizing a "Harlem Shake" video at *The Clarion-Ledger* and putting the thing on YouTube, Facebook and the media group's website did it, though.

It can also involve telling crazy family stories, a sure-fire method of offspring embarrassment. My thought on crazy stories involving children's antics is that if they do the antics, then they should have to deal with the crazy stories later.

It is payback, after all. Young parents act like hellions in public places and embarrass their parents, so it is only fitting that parents get to be an embarrassment for those same children a decade or so later.

My children are probably nervous that I write for a living and blog regularly. They should be.

It's similar to what my oldest Dear Son once told me when I said I didn't know whether to be grateful that he and I had the kind of relationship where he felt comfortable telling me stories about college life or horrified at what he was telling me. He replied that I should be grateful that he has the good sense not to tell me everything.

They should be grateful for the crazy stories I haven't shared.

Just being around breathing can embarrass a teenager. One of my Dear Sons used to duck down in the car when I was driving him somewhere. Never mind that he was not old enough to drive a car, and even if he had been, he wouldn't have had enough money to buy a car. Somehow, it was mortifying to be seen with his mama.

Also, there were rules. At the mall, I had to walk several feet away from him, lest people think we knew each other.

Once, all I did was hold up a shirt on a hanger and call his name. I was then told not to use his name in public, a dead giveaway for us knowing each other and me having carried him for nine months, which is another embarrassing fact.

Teenagers like to think they landed on Earth just like they are. Any other way of getting here, as in being born and being a baby and then a young child, might prove to be embarrassing.

I found this all amusing and used it to great advantage. All I had to do was threaten to kiss him and tell him "I love you" in front of his high school, and I could get him to do pretty much anything I wanted.

But that's pretty minor, in terms of embarrassing children.

To really embarrass them, you have to live with a lot of laughter and joy and energy. You have to jump off the high dive and holler all the way down. You have to dance in public and wear low-rise jeans. You have to laugh out loud and sing loud to the pop station on the radio when there are other people in the car.

Being an embarrassment means you might have to rollerskate and not act your age and make a public display of all your affections.

You might have to do things that are daring and that scare you a little, but in a good way.

Think up a few of these things and do them with enthusiasm, and I promise you, your teenager will be devastatingly, horribly embarrassed.

But they'll get over it. And then they'll go on to embarrass your grandchildren. That's the kind of legacy we all want to leave.

MOM vs. MOM

Mothers can be incredibly kind and tender-hearted to everyone, it seems, except other mothers.

That may sound harsh. By writing that, I myself am hating on other mothers. I can't make the observation otherwise, but just know I did notice the irony.

It's just we mothers tend to have ideas about what other mothers' mothering and families should look like.

Are you ready? They should look like ours. Or mine. Or yours.

Or we figure the other mothers have it easy. Or her life is fun and mine is drudgery.

We're matching grass blade to grass blade, looking carefully to see whose grass is greener, not noticing that we have our own greenery that might thrive with a little water and Miracle-Gro.

Moms who stay home vs. the moms who work. Single moms vs. married moms. They make for good daytime-talk-show fodder or articles for women's magazines, but as far as real life is concerned, there are better things we could be doing with our thoughts.

I've managed to make a tour through staying at home, working multiple jobs, being a married mom and being a single mom, and now that I have been there and didn't get any T-shirts because there were no souvenir stands, I can talk about them all.

Here is the deal: None of these lifestyles are the sweet life you think they might be. None are completely awful, either. They all have plusses, and they all have their drawbacks. Nobody's life is all princess without a little pre-Fairy Godmother Cinderella thrown in.

I didn't have a whole lot of choice in going from a married mom to a single one, but I can tell you that in the case of moms who work vs. moms who stay home, both are choices made based on what each family's needs are.

Working moms don't all wear power suits and heels and chair board of directors meetings. Maybe some do, but most don't. Some days at the office are fun and fulfilling and energizing, and others just aren't. By a long shot.

Stay-at-home moms don't all bake cookies and curl with their children for family time after the kiddos come bouncing off the school bus. OK, sometimes that happens, but not all the time. It's just like days at the office. Some days are heartwarming and wonderful, affirming everything good in this world. Other days the kids shave the dog, you manage to lock yourself out of the house in the rain, and Satan possesses the household plumbing.

The thing I missed when I was a stay-at-home mom? Adult conversation. Junior Auxiliary meetings were the only thing between me and insanity some days.

Nobody has it good all the time, and yet there exists the fallacy that one size fits all when it comes to mothering, and not all who hold that idea are mothers.

Once a supervisor, a man, had the questionable judgment to tell me that if I really loved my children, I would be at home with them instead of working. I was thinking two thoughts: "But then our home would be a box next to the Dumpster," and "Should I call the nearest EEOC office?"

Working mothers love their children every bit as much as the mothers who stay home. Both working moms and stay-at-home moms bring home pizza for dinner some nights because they are too exhausted to do anything else. The homes of stay-at-home moms and working moms are trainwrecks at times. June Cleaver is not a real person, but then neither is Claire Huxtable. Nobody's got a clean house, well-

51

behaved children, a great career and a charmed life every day.

Married moms don't all have great marriages. Some do, and I wish I could say those ladies are the majority. Based on statistics, about half do and others not so much, and that is probably realistic with a dose of optimism.

Single moms don't all have exciting social lives. I found it laughable that someone might think that after I became a single mom I did because I have spent more New Year's Eves sitting home than out and about. Sometimes my date is the sofa and a remote control, and don't knock it. That can be a pretty nice evening.

The married moms I knew wanted to hear all about my time on Match.com. "Where did you go to dinner? What was your date like? What did he wear? What did you wear? Did he call you later? What did he say?"

It was like the conversations I had at middle-school girls' sleepovers, only on dating instead of about talking to the cute boy in the hall at school.

I think the novelty might have been that I could get the benefits of date night without actually having to deal with the care and feeding of a husband the rest of the week.

Meanwhile, I was thinking how lucky these women are to have their husbands to come home to instead of listening to small talk from people they barely knew. They have someone to share dinner with each night, someone to talk to, someone to fall asleep with. They have someone who will look out for them and love them. They're incredibly blessed, even if they do have to deal with whiskers in the sink some mornings. I envy them, and funny, but I think some envy me back.

The truth is that we mamas all have it good. And we all have some rough patches to travel, too. No one's life is easy or perfect, or really, that different, so no one needs to envy another.

Kindness and tender-heartedness are in order, as we moms have much more in common than we think.

HELICOPTERS AND TIGERS

A businessman friend of mine noted a trend.

Not a huge one, but still disturbing.

Some parents, it seems, call the person their college-graduate child has just interviewed with for that all-important first job. They call and interview the boss, he said. You know, to find out if this person is worthy of working alongside their twenty-three-to-twenty-five-year-old baby. They ask about money, they ask about surroundings, office culture, probably even what kind of coffee is in the pot.

"The first time I got one of those calls, that poor child's resume would be in the circular file," he said. "Hiring that applicant would mean that I'd have to find another desk for his mama."

The fact that enough mamas (and daddies—let's not leave them out) do this sort of thing to make it a trend, to make it news for at least one business publication, means that the helicopters are airborne. Cue "Flight of the Valkyries."

A Helicopter Mom is one of those moms who hover, just like a you-know-what, over her children. She's the mother peeping in the schoolhouse window on the first day of kindergarten. She follows her child like a shadow at the park playground, never more than two feet away. She all but takes the ACT and the SAT for her child, and when his grades aren't up to par, it is the fault of the teacher and the educational system at large, never the child.

There was another Helicopter Mom story that made the news recently, this one about a mother who required her daughter to leave Skype on while she slept in her dorm room so she could watch her sleep.

Helicopter Moms are not to be confused with the phenomena of Tiger Moms. In the book *Battle Hymn of the Tiger Mother,* Amy Chua makes the case for a strict approach. Several of the Dear Sons' friends have Tiger Moms. A "B" for the nine weeks would mean grounding. A "B" for the year would mean summer school. Violin or piano lessons are mandatory. Sports are not. Making A's should be like breathing—constant.

Unlike the Helicopter Mom, who values her baby's self esteem above pretty much anything else in the universe, the Tiger Mom sees a child's self esteem as something to be earned by performance. No TV. Friends and sleepovers, not so much. Perfection is pushed. And pushed and shoved.

Now meet the Dolphin Dads. With authors such as Shawn Achor in *The Happiness Advantage* researching the happy effects of being happy, it was bound to happen. Dolphin dads are happy. They take a light approach. Happy kids are successful kids, the theory goes.

The animals and the flying machine are spawned from love. However lax the Dolphin Dad might be. However creepy the Helicopter Mom is. However tyrannical the Tiger Mom can become. It's all inspired by love.

I am thinking the way to go is to be a Human Mom. One who makes all kinds of mistakes but apologizes after messing up. She does the best she can. Her kids aren't perfect, and she's not either, but everyone's trying, most of the time. Or some days, some of the time. Any of the time is good.

That mom hugs frequently, laughs loudly, and frequently and loves hard. But err, and she might be on you like white on rice, as the saying goes.

She doesn't track her children's movements unless they need tracking.

Her children learn to do things on their own, and more than a few times, they learn by making mistakes. And when they do make those inevitable errors, they know where to go and whose shoulder to cry on.

She holds things together and thinks she's working herself out of a job.

Which is silly, because her children know she's irreplaceable.

That's the mom I want to be.

BECAUSE I SAID SO

"But, whyyyyy?"

Those may be the two most annoying words that ever have left a child's lips. For maximum annoyance, the "why" needs to be at least two syllables, with the "y" trailing off into a whine.

"But, whyyyyy?"

And the answer is the one that should be taught in college philosophy classes. It is simplistic, yet effective, if your word carries any weight at all.

"Because I said so.''

How many times did I hear that growing up? Exactly as many times as I *but-whyyyyed* my parents.

Those came in pairs, just like cause and effect.

But, whyyyyy? was the cause, and *Because I said so* was the effect.

Following with another *But, whyyyyy?* was the ultimate folly when I was a child. Only acting like a hellion in church would get you to the proverbial woodshed faster. More cause, more effect.

One *But, whyyyyy?* was allowed. Two or more *But, whyyyyys?* and it was like you were asking for a knot to be yanked in your tail.

Did I *But, whyyyyy?* my parents? Of course.

I am a journalist by trade. Asking "But, whyyyyy?'' to authority figures is in our DNA. Plus, all children want to know why, especially when it comes to something they may not be hopping up and down to do. This is when the unique pronunciation of the multi-syllabled "whyyyy''comes in.

But I also knew that once my daddy said "Because I said so,'' that was the end of it. I could have pushed it to maybe one more *But, whyyyyy?* with my mama, but that was about it.

Have I been *But, whyyyyyed?* by my own children? It only stands to reason that the girl who "But, whyyyyyed?" her parents into aggravation on a daily basis would grow up to have children who'd do the exact same thing to her. God does have a sense of humor, and this is just the sort of thing that would be laughed about in heaven, and I am convinced my mama and daddy have to be in on the joke

And of course, when my children say, "But, whyyyyy?'' I respond with "Because I said so.''

Sometimes they get a real explanation so whatever I told them to do makes sense, and most of the time, they don't want that much information. You can see the thought "Forget I asked" forming in their minds. A good "Because I said so'' is really all they want to hear some days.

The "Because I said so'' can be reassuring. As long as a mama has a "Because I said so" in her arsenal, she can bluff her way into convincing her offspring that she knows what she is doing. "Because I said so'' is wisdom talking. It restores order to the world.

Can you imagine a "Because I said so'' coming out of the mouths of Charlton Heston, James Earl Jones or Morgan Freeman? Nobody would dare to ask *But, whyyyyy?* after hearing that once. Clint

Eastwood would have a new catch phrase if he uttered the words, "Because I said so.''

An additional *But, whyyyyy?* won't send the offender looking for a switch at our house. Instead, they get the long explanation and wish they'd have had to look for a switch.

"Because I said so'' can be more than just a way to shush questions and get children in line. It shows the weight of a mama's word.

"But, whyyyyy?''

"Because I said so.''

If it works when a child questions why something has to be done, or done a certain way, then "Because I said so'' ought to work in other ways, too.

A good "Because I said so" shows no wavering. Mama spoke it, and so it is. So if mama means business on random issues of life, how much more does she mean it when she says, "You can do it. I know you can."

"You are my treasure.''

"You can do anything you put your mind to.''

"You can be anything you want."

"I love you."

But, whyyyyy? might cross a child's mind, just out of habit, because they do say that quite often.

Why, baby? Because I said so.

MANNING UP

Some things come easily to mothers.

Hugs. We are natural born huggers. Kissers, too. We are kissing fools, and it's a good thing, since it is a scientific fact that mother kisses can and do cure all manner of boo-boos.

My second son once accused me of not loving him.

"Sweetheart," I said. "I love you with all my heart."

About two years old at the time, he said, "You know I don't like kisses, and you're always kissing my face."

It's the price he had to pay for being loved fiercely, I told him at the time. And for being cheek-pinchingly cute.

He was being a boy and hating the mushy stuff, but he was facing down nature. We mamas comfort. We love. We build up. It's part of being a mama.

But sometimes, mamas have to man up and be on the tough side. My own mama did.

I was about thirty at the time and had just moved to Jackson from West Point. I was taking on a job that was stretching my abilities and making me grow. In other words, it shoved me right out of my comfort zone all day every day.

Not only that, but my husband and sons were three hours away during the week, as we wanted the kids to finish the semester and get the house ready to sell. So during the week, I worked hard, miles

59

away from comfortable, and missed my children desperately.

And then my dad had a health scare. We thought he might have had cancer, but it turned out he was plenty healthy. We didn't know that at the time, though. At the time, Dad was complaining about my mother fussing over him and me worrying about him. Such is the lot of a man outnumbered by a wife and daughter.

I was back home on a weekend to visit, and was telling my mother all about this—that my job was hard and that I just knew my boss hated me and I didn't know anyone and how maybe I should just pack up the apartment and go home. I could find another job, I said, and maybe I should be closer for her and my daddy. I wasn't being a good mother, I said, being so far away from the boys, who were then six and eight.

Blah, blah, blah. No matter what I said, it wasn't sinking in. My mama was having none of it.

"You're making excuses to quit," she said. "You are where you need to be and deserve to be. You have to stay. Do it for your family. They'll be better off because you did this. You will get the hang of it."

You're not about to come home, she said.

Quitting was something that was near heresy at our house. You could master something and move to the next challenge, but quitting something because it was hard was just not done.

"You are not quitting," she said. Period. That was that.

Although people around town knew my mother as one of the sweetest women in town, she did have a side to her that was not to be questioned. I got to see that side of her that evening.

And I got to show that side to one of mine.

He was a brand new twenty-four-year-old manager, and he was learning that ironclad truth of business, that being a manager is difficult. It is not about putting your feet up and hollering for your secretary to come take a memo.

My boy—meant only as a term of endearment and not as a description of maturity—called me one day about 1 o'clock. He had just made a move to work in Kansas City, some 10 hours away from home. He was moving into a new place, a new job and a new office. Nothing about his life was easy.

"I want to come home," he said. "I could move back in and go back to school. I have so many things to do, I don't know what to do first. This is too hard."

And as much as I wanted to say, "Baby, of course you can come home," as much as I would have loved to have him back under my roof, I couldn't. It was time for me as a mama to man up, but with a mother's touch. I learned from the best.

"Have you had lunch?" I asked. "Stop where you are and go get something to eat. Things will look better then. Then call your boss and tell him you need help on setting priorities."

Love? Thick and sweet like syrup.

Care? Constant.

But quitting? Just like my mama, I was having none of it.

MOTHERS OF SONS

God does indeed have a sense of humor. One of the manifestations of God's divine comedic work is that mothers raise sons. While they're a gift and a joy, sons don't always make sense to their mamas. It's on account them being little men.

When they're boys, it is a battle of wits, mama vs. son, and mamas are at a severe disadvantage. Why? Because they can think of things to do that won't even enter a mama's mind.

Only a little boy would think to jump from a bed to a ceiling fan, swinging around on its blades until the wood and metal wilted like flower petals.

Only brothers would come up with the idea of putting a frog in each mailbox on the street. I heard them laughing about it, anticipating frogs hopping into their neighbors' faces. What they didn't anticipate was that the frogs would roast in those mailboxes since it was a Mississippi summer. They also didn't anticipate being overheard.

So we went out, the three of us, me holding the flashlight while one by one, the frogs were freed.

Years ago, when I knew everything, which was before I had children, I used to think that boys would be boys and girls would be girls because they were conditioned to be that way. Boys were rough from roughhousing, and they played with trucks because trucks were given to them. If they were given a dollhouse, they'd play much like little girls would.

Well, not exactly.

My friend Katie's sons were playing while we were turning Madison United Methodist Church into a medieval castle for Vacation Bible School. They got the run of a Sunday school classroom with toys, and the three boys found a doll house.

They played with it as only little boys would. They filled it with plastic dinosaurs, Tyrannosaurus Rexes with teeth bared, brontosauruses watching TV, and triceratops or one of his cousins, relaxing by the fire. There was a motorcycle in the foyer.

Boys are just different than girls, and girls grow up to be mamas. So, of course, our sons are not always going to make sense to us, any more than mamas make sense to them.

But we mamas wind up teaching them to be men. Which is something none of us mamas have any experience being.

"I finally got mine to pee standing up," said one friend of mine going through potty training.

I wouldn't care if mine were standing on their heads as long as it went where it was supposed to, but some of the things we teach our boys are just foreign. My son needed to know how to tie a tie for his senior Class Day, and I would have been lost if it had not been for YouTube. I've taught them how to mow the yard, but I have yet to sell it to them like Tom Sawyer. Being a good date, tried on that one, succeeding more than I've failed, I hope. They've figured out shaving on their own without asking and without too much blood loss.

The best things we mamas can teach our sons are how to love and how to think, to be honest and treat others as they would want to be treated, that being strong means helping others, that being a man has to include at least as much tenderness as tenacity and grit.

A MISSISSIPPI MAMA

There's no mama like a Mississippi mama.

Why? Well, there actually are plenty of mamas like us, but since I am from Mississippi, I like to think we're special. Like there is something in the water, although there may be, now that I think about it.

Being a Mississippi mama is being a steel magnolia. To say that the term "steel magnolia" is worn out is taking the term "worn out" down to the basement level of worn-outedness. It's patches on your patches' patches worn out.

But there really is no other way to explain it. Mamas, and by the powers vested in me (just kidding, I have none), I pronounce all mamas, no matter where they are from, as being honorary Mississippi mamas, have an unmistakable blend of softness and authority. They're sweet, yet a force to be reckoned with. They love hard, are gracious and friendly, but God help you if you hurt one of their babies.

Being a Mississippi mama means you take care of business. You probably own the business, run the business or at least keep things going so the bosses can't figure out what they'd do without you. Or maybe you run your home like a Fortune 500 company.

It means you pay the bills, and more than likely either know how to fix a thing or two or know how to hire or sweet-talk your man into doing it.

Mississippi mamas take care of their own. My own mama used to love reading about the woman in Proverbs 31, a lady who, frankly, gives us all a tough row to hoe. She clothed her family, was a smart businesswoman, cared for her entire household and laughed about the future because she didn't worry about a thing. She was a supermom before anyone thought about such a thing.

I've read the theory that the Proverbs 31 woman was not just one person but a composite of women, and it figures that someone would think that. Mamas do tend to do the work of more than one person. For free, I might add.

I am pretty sure the lady in Proverbs 31 would qualify as a Mississippi mama, too.

Being the child of a Mississippi mama means you are taken care of. Dinner is on the table, although some nights it might come out of a pizza box, and you've got clothes, although they might be hand-me-downs. You've got a roof over your heard, although it might leak in a place or two.

Mississippi mamas will keep going no matter what, because the alternative isn't even in the realm of the thinkable. What would have most people horizontal is nothing to a Mississippi mama. We'd care for our babies even if our heads were half attached.

Mississippi mamas do expect a little something in return. How about a "yes, ma'am?" How about the groceries getting carried in without us asking? It just does my heart good when I see my teenage son mow the yard when he sees it needs to be done.

We expect some work. I know it's a four-letter word, but we'll throw it around anyway. Few things get Mississippi mamas as riled up as laziness. And a Mississippi mama knows all kinds of ways to yank a knot in the tails of their babies when they need it. Few, if any, involve a trip to the woodshed.

Mississippi mamas are tough. These magnolias don't wilt under pressure.

But no one can dole out tender, loving care like a Mississippi mama. Our love is thick, smooth and banana pudding sweet. Those we love are loved hard. They never escape our presence without an "I love you'' or sugar or something. Sugar for us is not just something that goes in the iced tea pitcher. Hugs and kisses.

One of our babies gets a sniffle, and we're on it. Broken heart? We're there with sympathy and ice cream. Our sugar can heal boo-boos from scraped knees to concussions.

It's all we can do, sometimes, to let our babies go out into the world, which is a rough place where hearts get broken and knees get scraped. But we let them. We cry over it, whether our babies are heading to the first day of kindergarten or the first day of college or the first day of the first job after graduation.

And we celebrate the firsts, even though it's not easy.

We love those who love our babies, and the family of a Mississippi mama is, like the universe, ever expanding. Family to us stretches to cousins, friends, coworkers. When Jesus said to love our neighbors, Mississippi mamas took that to heart. The whole world at times can be not only our neighbor, but could pull a chair up at our homes if only we had enough leaves to our dining tables.

There's no mama like a Mississippi mama? While each one of us is a unique blend of strength and tenderness, sugar and bite, by the grace of God, there's enough of us to go around.

EMERGENCY ROOMS

Are you a mother of sons?

Then you don't have to have watched "ER" back in the day to know what an emergency room is like. You're already been there. Quite a bit. And you will keep going until they hit the age where they are old enough to know better.

With sons, you'll be a frequent flyer to the ER.

Enough to offer the doctor a second opinion.

Enough to wonder if perhaps you should learn how to do stitches at home to save a few bucks.

Enough for them to know you by name when you come in.

Enough that you could be a consultant for any television show involving emergency rooms, boys under eighteen and falling off swings, monkey bars, and tree branches.

Dear daughters will have you going to the emergency room, too, but rarely as often as Dear sons do. Strange, but I am pretty sure this is the case outside of our family. It's really kind of amazing that baby boys make it to adulthood. They are like those thousands of little baby sea turtles trying to make it into the ocean. You just pray they all get there.

The world is a dangerous place for all of us, but danger is a boy magnet.

Getting stitches is a male rite of passage. It seems they all need to find a way to spring a good-sized leak, be it from an elbow to the head in basketball, or like mine, falling off monkey bars, playing with a shovel or walking into the edge of a door. Those really don't make great stories, though. They're going to have to think up some good stories to tell any girls who happen to ask about their scars.

It doesn't matter to us mamas how these things happen. Blood's blood.

There's a reason the rest of us non-medical types haven't pursued careers in medicine. There's a shortage of nurses because it takes a special person to deal with blood. The rest of us want to throw up, pass out or throw up and then pass out.

And needles. Did I mention those?

Your precious sweet baby who's sprung a leak is lying in the treatment room, and you, as his devoted mama, are there to comfort him and tell him everything is going to be all right. And then the needle comes out to deaden the area to be stitched back together.

I don't know about y'all, but in the vernacular of northeast Mississippi, I liked to died. We leave the "have" off. It's quicker that way.

Here comes the great big ol' needle, about to pierce my sweet crying baby's skin, and I liked to (have) died.

Childbirth is easier than watching your baby get stitches. Not only did I hit the "liked to died" stage, I went on to the "wanted to climb the walls" and hit "Oh, dear God."

The sweet babies get the stitches, but we mamas are the ones who are light-headed.

And stitches are the minor stuff.

I passed by everything until I got to "Oh, dear God'' when broken bones were involved.

Broken bone are usually preceded by "Hey, watch this.'' Anything that happens after those words are said never ends well.

Both "Hey, watch this'' moments in our family were followed with trips to the ER made by a frantic mama driving and a howling sweet baby in the back. It hurt to even look at them.

And then there are the concussions. Dear sons are lots of fun. You don't know what fun is until you have a kid who's fallen out of a tree, doesn't know how he got back in the house and just wants to go to sleep.

When you have one of those, you go past "Oh, Dear God'' and start praying to all religions of the world simultaneously, hoping one of them is going to get you through.

You go past being the soul of civility that you usually are and, upon arriving at the emergency room, you run out of the car, lean in the door and scream, "I've got a kid with a head injury!" That tends to raise a few eyebrows.

Sons do tend to make you think they are just trying not to remain above ground. They get these nifty bodies when they are born, all new and fresh and healthy. And then they spend their entire boyhood and sometimes part of their manhood trying to wreck them. You'd think they were in a demolition derby, only with their bodies instead of cars.

Children do make you a more spiritual person. They can make you exclaim, "Oh, my Lord" with the things they come up with doing. Boys tend to have a real affinity for this. Usually it involves climbing tall things and gravity, or the physics of going fast and meeting immovable objects.

I think, since we mamas of sons are going to be spending time in the emergency room, there should be a special place for moms to just get through the experience. Dark chocolate and Diet Coke should be involved, along with a meditation tape that will help us breathe and think about our "happy place." Or maybe a nice, soothing poster of a beach scene that we can look at instead of the blood and the needles.

There'd be less passing out that way.

MOTHER SUPERPOWERS

One of my sons gave me a coffee mug for my birthday inscribed with the words:

I'm a Mom . . . What's your super power?

The sentiment springs from a polka-dotted ceramic surface.

It's the sort of thing that makes you laugh at first, and then reflect. Moms might indeed have super powers.

Oh, sure, we go under cover, just like Batman is really Bruce Wayne and Superman is really Clark Kent. The world could not handle all our motherly super powers if we were just throwing them out there like bags of pork rinds on shelves at the Walmart. We have to be incognito.

But super powers? Of course we have them.

My daughter, young at the time, was brushing my hair one Sunday afternoon, paying special attention to the back.

"Baby, what are you doing?" I asked after a certain amount of rooting around.

"Looking for the eyes in the back of your head."

I told her the truth. That the eyes in the back of my head were invisible to children.

Of course, I have eyes in the back of my head. All mothers do. We get them during childbirth. By the time the baby is strapped into the car seat for the first time, we've got a personal back-up camera just like the minivan.

Mamas also have super hearing.

Many is the time when I have stopped mid-conversation, a glass of tea halfway to my lips.

"Do you hear that?" I'd ask.

"What? I don't hear anything."

"It's too quiet," I'd say. "The kids are up to something."

I'd track down the ominous sounds of silence, and sure enough, someone would be up to no good. Playing with matches or running with scissors might have ensued had my super mama hearing not kicked in.

Magical spit. It is also another mama super power. Mother spit can cure all manner of boo-boos. If enough research was done, it might reveal that mama spit could cure cancer.

"Mama!" I've heard some child of mine wail, holding some scrape or bump. "Kiss it!"

Muah. All better. And after the lesser treatments of antibiotic and a bandage, sniffling child was close to good as new.

Mama spit is dual purpose. It also is a cowlick tamer for boys. Lick the palm, smooth the hair.

"Did you just rub spit in my hair?" one of my boys asked incredulously.

"Your hair was sticking up."

We mamas also know a thing or two about pinching pennies and stretching dollars. Many of us should have Ph.Ds in economics for keeping a roof over everyone's head and food on the table.

We don't have invisible airplanes like Wonder Woman did, but those are over-rated. Number one, if I can lose visible car keys and have problems finding my car in the supermaket parking lot, how often would I lose an invisible airplane?

And if you are visible yet flying an invisible airplane, you know anyone looking into the sky would be able to see right up your skirt.

Bullet-catching bracelets might be handy, but only for those mamas on the police force and in the military.

Being able to have speed like Flash, or a tool belt like Batman . . . both would be handy to possess. Outrunning a todder or my dog or just sprinting into work on time for an 8 a.m. meeting . . . that would be a super power indeed, plus it would be pretty awesome at the elementary school's annual 5K run.

And the tool belt Batman has. I could deal with one of those since I can't seem to keep up with a Phillips head screwdriver or a wrench at home. They're there until needed.

Being able to shoot webs might seem to be awesome, but somebody has to clean those up. Sweeping cobwebs from the ceiling is just another chore, plus being bitten by a radioactive spider to gain that power would probably leave a mark.

And no mama wants to wear Spandex on the outside of her clothes. Spanx are our secret superhero clothes, and when they hold everything together, they are indeed miraculous.

What mamas do makes those other super powers pale in comparison.

We can bend the space and time continuum, and not only for threatening to knock wayward children into the middle of next week. How we pack twenty-five hours into twenty-four is nothing short of, well, super. We're mothers, daughters, significant others, friend, employees, supervisors, students (because we never stop learning), and we still manage to get the laundry done.

We run a taxi service, heal the boo-boos mentioned above, plan events, cook dinners, clean rooms and save the world for those we love multiple times daily.

We don't give up. We bend time to our will. We care for ourselves spiritually, physically and mentally not so much because it makes us better, but because it makes us better for those we hold in our hearts.

Mamas love hard, laugh hard and hold tenderly.

Yeah, those are my super powers.

What are yours?

BASEBALL MOMS

Mississippi State University went to the finals of the College World Series not long ago. As I watched those young men in maroon take the field, my first thought was how proud we should be of them. My second thought was that it took a lot of crazy parents to get them that far.

Yes, baseball parents are crazy. Go ahead. Write me letters and call me in protest. I have been a baseball mom, so I have been there and have the crazy T-shirt to prove it.

It starts with Tee Ball. Little boys and a few girls hit a baseball off a tee, and if they can hit the ball, they then run the bases. Getting them to run to first instead of third by the end of the season is a small triumph. No official score is kept, but unofficially? Unofficially, those kids might as well have been in the College World Series, because the Tee Ball dads were following the score that closely. It was all they could do to not gnaw on the middle-schooler umpire when a bad call was made.

The baseball moms are just as much into the game as the dads, if not moreso. Once a Tee Ball mom started pounding her fist into Baby Daddy's shoulder while he was standing next to her waiting for our son's game to start and the game being played to end.

"RUN!!! RUN!!! . . . Oh, I am so sorry . . ."

He just stood there, stunned, and made a mental note never to stand next to a Tee Ball mom he wasn't married to at the time.

Then there are the team moms. These are some dedicated women. They figure out who will make cupcakes decorated like baseballs, and the uber team moms make the things themselves just to make the rest of us look bad. The team moms make sure there is Gatorade after games, round up trophies for the end-of-the-season pizza party, which they organize, and chaperone the team to see minor league games. The best team moms arrange for the team to take the field with the Jackson Generals or the Diamond Kats in those years before the Mississippi Braves came to Pearl. Mine even danced as he stood next to the third baseman one year.

Team momming, and yes, it is an action verb, is work, but it's also fun with a little crazy mixed in. I miss those days at times, and then I remember the time I left a platter of cupcakes on top of my car and drove off, leaving the driver behind me dodging cupcakes and scraping frosting off with his windshield wipers.

It is sweet, in those Tee Ball and later Coach Pitch days. The parents are crazy … crazy about their kids. They all want a collection of happy baseball memories for their children. They want all homeruns in the bottom of the ninth with bases loaded and no memories of strike-outs unless their children are pitchers, They want trophies for them all because each child's a winner.

They cheer loud. "Come on, boy, GIVE IT A RIDE!!"

The boy doesn't swing.

"That's OK. Good eye. Good eye."

"FIRE UP! Let's see some heat!!"

And that's from the moms. My oldest once told me to stop yelling when he came up to bat.

"You're embarrassing me, mom . . ."

So I then would keep quiet, saying prayers for a base hit.

Then the craziness gets more intense. There were select teams, and baseball bats that cost as much as a car payment.

Baby Daddy began to have dreams of his boys signing college scholarships to play ball. Who knows? They could be in the pros.

He wasn't alone. All the baby daddies had these dreams for their boys.

"After my son plays on the middle school team …" a fellow baby daddy said.

"You know he has to try out, right?" Baby Daddy said. "No one gets to just get on the team."

"It's a formality. I want him to head to an SEC school after middle school and high school."

It was a sure thing, the other baby daddy said.

Our son tried out and didn't make the middle school team. The other boy didn't either.

"He was crying, Mom."

About then, the craziness had become, for some, more about the parents' dreams, or about the parents, than it was about wanting a season of happiness for their kids.

"It's not fun anymore," mine said to me one day. "I don't want to play this spring."

"You sure?"

"Yeah."

"OK, then."

That liked to have killed Baby Daddy. First one son stopped playing, then the other. There was a huge void in his life that spring. It was the first year in a long, long time that we didn't have a boy playing left field, short or third.

For the first time in a decade, I wasn't going to have a baseball mom tan that started at the hem of my shorts and ended at the flip-flop strap.

There was no more talk of baseball glories of the future at our house, and that, after a period of mourning, was OK. Life went on, and it turns out that life is about more than just hitting the ball.

It was time for our family to live in the sanity of the off season the whole year. After all, only a select few crazy parents get to Omaha.

MOTHERS AND DAUGHTERS

I had just become a mother of a daughter, and my mother, also the mother of a daughter, had a gift for me.

It was a wedding ring worn by the mother of a daughter, who grew up to be the mother of a daughter, otherwise known as my maternal great-grandmother.

"I love my choice," the inscription on the ring read on the inside of the plain, gold band, size five as the women in our family are small-handed.

The ring, passed from great-grandmother to grandmother to my mother, was then given to me because I had become the mother of a daughter. I was told to wear it for my daughter, so I can then pass it on to not just her but one day my granddaughter.

Being a mother of a daughter is an exclusive club. I had three sons before she came along, but I never heard about the ring until I joined the club with the lady my kids called Grandma.

I'm not sure what would have happened had I not had the youngest, our Dear Daughter, but she came along and the ring had two more women in the family to travel to, myself and her.

Being a mother of a daughter is not unlike passing along a family treasure. There are so many things you want to hand down, and some you hand down whether you want to or not.

You want to give a daughter the gift of family, because so many times, it is the mamas and sisters and aunts who are the glue that holds families together. Equal parts tenderness and strength, because she'll need a balance of both. Laughter, because a sense of humor can get you through life smiling. Daring, because brave girls grow up to be brave women.

Try as you might to hand those down consciously, they get passed along in the everyday, in the getting through life, when she's watching you when you're not looking.

And some things get passed along because God has a sense of humor. It is payback.

So many times, I will listen to myself and realize I sound just like my mother when my daughter acts just like I did growing up. The first time you realize both of those dynamics are happening, it is a sobering thought.

It's just like the first time you looked into the mirror first thing in the morning and noticed that your eyelid is crinkling and you realize, "My mother's eyelid used to do that crepey thing in the morning." And then you realize you've graduated from blemish cream to age-fighting moisturizer.

Or the time when family holiday gatherings are at your house instead of at your mama's.

The torch is passed. A Thanksgiving dinner here, a eyelid crease there and hearing the words, "If all your friends were jumping off a building, I suppose you'd want to do that, too," slip out of your mouth, and you realize you're a lot more like your mama than you ever thought you'd be.

How on earth did an artsy, nerdy, hard-headed girl like me wind up with a daughter who's also artsy, strong-willed and a lover of all things anime and "Doctor Who?"

And how did I start sounding like the voice of reason and practicality? When did I start using words like "shenanigans?" And advocating sensible shoes?

There was a time in my life, as in most girls' lives, when I didn't want to be anything like my mother. I reveled in all the differences. And she told me how she used to feel the same about her mother. They would argue, just as she and I would. She told me she used to wish she could take back all the harsh words she said, and I wish I could take back all the ugliness I handed her in my younger, less patient, more foolish days. Yet there was always love, even though daughters sometimes try to wrest the torch out of their mama's hands.

My own Dear Daughter rolls her eyes at me. She thinks we couldn't be more different. I like *Downton Abbey* more than sci-fi, and she doesn't get how I can read nonfiction and run for pleasure.

We don't always see eye to eye. If we did, it would be a first among mothers and daughters everywhere. Even though there are similarities between the Dear Daughter and I that she doesn't want to admit, looking at the world the same way is difficult. Mamas have a thing called experience.

Sometimes we don't want our daughters to make the mistakes we made. Having a daughter can feel like a chance to, if not make the right decisions the first time around, to at least influence better decisions in round two.

There is always the love, whether our daughters' choices are ones we mamas would choose for them or whether they go their own way. Hint: They usually do the latter, and that is for the best.

Mamas and their daughters are different, and those differences should be celebrated even as we carry the similarities around, sometimes storing them away in a jewelry box, sometimes wearing them like an heirloom ring.

ZONING OUT

My second Dear Son was rattling on about something. What, I have no idea.

He was a teenager then, and I had managed to tune him out and was thinking about something a million miles away.

"Mom, have you been listening to me?" he asked.

"I'm sorry, baby," I said. "I was zoning you out."

You would have thought I'd have said, "Sorry, I was killing kittens," the way he reacted. He was shocked—shocked, I tell you—and indignant.

Like he never zoned me out.

Kids do that all the time to their mamas.

I sound like the teacher in the Peanuts cartoons. Charlie Brown asks her a question, and the unseen teacher replies, "Whawhawahwah."

I know that plenty of times I was speaking normal words, but what was coming into my kids' ears was "Whawhawhawha."

My children seldom hear well when it involves chores, but let me unwrap a hidden candy bar, and they suddenly can hear like dogs. Their hearing is selective.

Zoning out children is not the worst thing you can do. It can preserve your sanity, for one. It can keep you from finding a substance to abuse. Like Calgon, it can take you away. It is cheaper than a babysitter or a vacation.

But try, mamas, to keep yourself in the moment most of the time. Your days as a hands-on, in-the-trenches mama are fleeting, so don't zone out half of them. You might miss something.

I used to hear that my kids would be grown up the next time I turned around. And it may take a little longer than turning around, but not much. The days are long, but the years are short.

Don't zone out, or something good will happen, and you'll miss it.

Being a mama is all about being in the moment. You have to watch as many moments as you can, because you never know when the good stuff will happen. That first step is never scheduled. Kids never give you adequate notice when they're going to do something worthy of writing down in their baby book.

Being a mother is all about being spontaneous, all about the moment and going with the flow. You've heard people, in reviewing movies, say, "I laughed, I cried?" You will do all that and more in motherhood once you are engaged and in tune. But you have to be there and not simply going through the motions.

Put your iPhone and tablet away. Stop checking your email. Go play with your children. When they're in college, your girls will no longer want to play Barbies with you.

A messy house isn't going anywhere. It will still be there, but your children won't. They keep insisting on growing up.

One day, your house will be clean, which will mean that your either have a live-in housekeeper or that your children have grown up and moved away. Don't ever put off enjoying the company of your children until you have a clean house, because we both know that's probably not happening.

I can toss the iPhone aside, and putting aside housework is no problem at all. What is hard, at times, is to tune in and actively listen. Whether it's daydreaming or thinking about what we need at the supermarket, thoughts can keep your brain so occupied that even though you seem like you are listening, you're really not taking anything in.

The child walks off, and I'm left wondering, "Now what did she just say?"

That's not good. I don't want the Dear Daughter wheeling out of the driveway with all her stuff in a U-Haul, on her way to being a grown-up, and me thinking, "What just happened?" I want to have lots of memories, and I don't remember for beans when I am zoning out the children.

It's not possible to be fully engaged all the time and be human, but do the best you can. The best memories happen that way.

Part 3

Growing up

CRIME AND PUNISHMENT

When I was a child, there were two schools of thought on the discipline of children. There were those who favored paddles and those who were in the belt crowd. There were no spare-the-rod advocates back in the day.

That is too bad, really, because I have come to understand that paddlings, spankings and otherwise whipping the tar out of children is just not that effective.

For starters, these don't last that long. When my older two dear sons had infractions in middle school and high school, I got a call from them, asking me to please OK them getting corporal punishment. The reason was that the alternative to that was the dreaded ISD, or in-school detention. In ISD Land, students have to sit there all day not talking to anyone. Mine were totally fine with a short paddling as opposed to a day-long ordeal.

Another problem with whooping the tar our of your child is that your child is growing every day. You are not. One day, your child will be your size or larger. If you don't have that child hanging onto your every word by any other means than waylaying him, eventually you will have no other means of getting his attention. Threatening to paddle a six-foot boy when you are five foot two is just laughable. And your child will be the one doing the laughing.

Now there is also the problem of hitting to make an impact, because this is not a good lesson to hand out. "If you don't stop hitting other kids, I am going to wear you out by hitting your backside with a board. "

See how ridiculous that is?

But mainly there is just a total lack of creativity in corporal punishment. There is no tailoring of the sentence to fit the crime. And the kids know what they will get, because of that lack of creativity, so they weigh it out. I know, because I did this and so did pretty much every kid I grew up with. Would the crime be worth the risk of a paddling? Maybe yes, maybe no.

But if you are creative about it, your child would have no idea what would be coming. It just ruins the risk assessment, the weighing of the crime vs. the punishment, because the punishment is an unknown.

And it can be horrible.

There are some punishments that are just to terrible to risk. Such as the one I have only threatened mine with. That's right . . . having to hold your sibling's hand in the car all the way home. We were about forty-five minutes from the house when the youngest Dear Son and the Dear Daughter decided to go to war. They sounded worse than the worst of bad marriages.

I did not care who started it, who was right or who was wrong. I just wanted two kids to hush so I would not lose my mind. So the deal was that the car was not moving, the key would not turn, not even the air conditioner or radio would run, until I got a big ol' slice of quiet. And if they continued to fight, they would have to hold hands with each other all forty-five minutes home. I have a rear-view mirror and eyes in the back of my head, so I could keep them honest in case they wanted to let go.

Guess what? I had two quiet kids. It turns out having to hold your younger sister's or older brother's hand must be like dipping your paw into a barrel of toxic waste.

Then there was the time the two older Dear Sons, elementary students at the time, could not stop insulting each other. They were calling each other everything but their given names, and I don't like insults being hurled about in our home. The world's a rough enough place without verbal assaults once you walk in the front door.

So, in one of my better, more creative days as a mother, I had them sit at the kitchen table. I gave them each a piece of paper and told them to number it from 1 to 20. They were not to get up until they wrote twenty nice things about each other.

What resulted was perhaps the funniest thing I ever read.

The pain they were going through in trying to be insulting while not being insulting was nothing short of hysterical.

They complimented each other on their "pretty" hair, and this is a first-class insult brother to brother. Fighting words.

They hailed each other for not having feet that stink too bad, for being potty trained, for not wetting the bed. For every genuine compliment, such as noting that one was good at drawing and the other played video games well, there were at least five that involved purported kind words about bathroom habits, stink or the lack thereof and being "pretty." No little boy wants to be called "pretty," but it was a word that would pass muster with me.

This will work, by the way, if your children lobbing verbal ugliness at each other are too young to write. Just have them say five nice things about each other face to face and then tell them to hug or at least shake hands.

You can't force them to think nice things, but you can at least get them to act semi-civilized. Plus, the awfulness of having to say nice things to your sibling's face will make them think twice about verbalizing all the nasty thoughts about said sibling that runs through the brain. I suppose I should be happy that they don't say everything they think.

Another awful punishment is the clipping of wings, or bicycles, or cars. When a child breaks a rule about cycling, or later on, about driving, the punishment has to fit the crime.

Once, to get the attention of the oldest when he was riding too far away on his bicycle, Baby Daddy put up hooks and hung the cycle up for a week or so in the carport. Nothing like walking past your beloved cycle, but not being able to get it down to ride it.

Later, when some car rules were broken, I removed the battery of the car and hid it. I informed this same child that if he could find and install that battery, I would figure out what the distributor cap looked like and where it was, and then it would be gone. The car, a 10-year-old Saturn later dubbed the Landshark, sat there for a month, battery-less.

The younger two have since laughed about our time-out chair, but we had one, and they absolutely hated sitting in it, having to stare at a wall in the dining room while decent company watched TV.

Pretty soon, all that had to be done was mention the time-out chair. It was being used less and less, because the mere threat of it was enough to straighten up erring children.

And that, truly, is the secret to discipline. Your children actually don't have to be punished because, as long as they know the possibility of punishment exists, that it is a real thing, such as missing a favorite show, and not metaphorical, like being grounded until age forty, and that you are just crazy enough as a parent to follow through, then most of the time, they will mend their ways.

BACK TO SCHOOL

I remember my first day of school.

I was dressed in a red and blue polyester dress and had a blue book bag. Back then, no one carried backpacks. This looked like a first cousin to a briefcase, only from the low-rent neighborhood of the local Five and Dime. Inside, there were brand-new crayons, manila paper, fat first-grader pencils and paper with the dotted lines for penmanship.

My mama had her Kodak camera out, and to her credit, she put on a happy face. Maybe it was because I was a handful, or maybe it was because she had been a teacher in lower elementary grades before she married. She knew just how awful crying mothers of crying children can be.

At any rate, she never got all weepy when I started school each year. Not one grade. She was just happy about the new adventure. Most likely, more happy than I was. She might have been happy enough for both of us.

I didn't realize it at the time, but she was giving me a gift that I could pass along to my own children. It was the gift of enthusiastically letting go. She didn't always have this skill down pat, but then I struggle with it, too.

This week, my youngest Dear Son started high school. Just like 15-year-old boys do, he acted unfazed by it all. Fifteen-year-old boys are like cats. Cats and teenage boys don't get ruffled, and they tend to temper any outbursts of joy with coolness.

And just like my mama, I didn't cry. Not even privately, and I really thought I would. I may be saving it up those emotions for Drivers' Ed.

I cried to myself in the middle of the night when the Dear Daughter was starting middle school, though. Not having a child in elementary school for the first time in forever seemed like it was worthy of some tears.

But this time, this year, no tears. Not even by-myself tears.

I think it was because he is as tall as I am. It's time he was a freshman, and I know how much fun high school will be. He and his friends pretended not to be excited, but their Instagram posts tell a different tale. High school, high school, high school.

I remember that excitement. It's something we should all wish for our children. It's like running alongside them when our babies are learning to ride bikes. When we let go, we do it with a little shove to send them on their way.

When they whoop and holler over riding on two wheels, we cheer, and when they fall—and they will—we're there with the Band-aids, kisses and pep talk. We dust them off and encourage them to get right back on.

My mama, on her best days, could do the letting go with a shove and a cheer, yet still be there. There's irony in that, I know, but motherhood is fraught with irony. The better job we mamas do, the more we work ourselves out of it.

To cry over children going to school is, in a way, a selfish thought, and we mamas try to keep those to a minimum. It is to wish them to be little boys and little girls forever. Never smarter than we are, never taller. They'd never make decisions we didn't approve of. They'd never drive cars, go on dates, major in basketry, smoke cigarettes, or drink beer. And as tempting as that might be to wish for our children at times, it's as if we'd be wishing them to not jump into this puddle called life. Sure, they will get their feet wet. They might slip and fall, and they'll definitely get muddy.

After all, we did.

To spare our children the messy parts of life and the challenges and the scraped knees and the first days of school is to take away all the graduations and victories and the joy of jumping and splashing.

They can't stay little forever, and our children are their own people with their own wills and thoughts. Anyone who's raised a two-year-old can tell you that.

You can't let a two-year-old set off on his own, although it can be tempting at times, and you can't cling to your high school student, either. Children need a little shove and a cheering section each year, a little bit more responsibility and challenge and independence along with those binders and backpacks, until they're off on their own, the ultimate in new adventures.

Don't worry. They'll still need their mamas. Nobody outgrows the need for love and wisdom and cheerleading and the occasional shove.

KIDS IN CHURCH

There was a time of retribution like no other in my growing-up years. It was when church let out.

At no other time in no other day did more children get more beatings, spankings, whippings and whatnot than after church.

Now let me preface this by saying our parents were not the "spare the rod" types. If you loved your children, the thinking back then was you would get to the seat of the problem. Rapidly. There were no time-outs back then. We kids would have loved those.

I am not an advocate of spanking children because I think there are more effective ways of communicating right and wrong than hitting. That sentence would have been laughed off the street in the South circa the early 1970s, though. And if one was to call one of those hiney-warmings child abuse, then I guess a whole town's worth of parents would have been locked up.

No, we kids all wound up being worn out at one time or another. It was only a question of when and where.

Usually, most waylayings happened once the 15th go-round of "Just as I am" was played and a couple of people rededicated their lives to Christ. The handshakings and greetings would begin as folks made their way to their cars in an effort to beat the Methodists to the Sunday buffet at the Southern Inn.

We kids would be walking out of the church together, and sure enough, some other child would be screaming in the parking lot. Probably several. It was the topic of discussion for us—who was getting a beating and what they did in church to deserve it.

Church misbehavior would get you a warm behind faster than setting fire to the school back then. It was a reflection on your parents' child-rearing in the public-est place in town. You didn't challenge authority too much more than acting like a heathen in church. It was like asking for the physical motivation to stand awhile.

We would witness someone wearing out their young'uns' backsides beside the family's Chevy Malibu and be thankful that our own badness, doodling, whispering and note-passing didn't cross the line that Sunday.

Our badness continued, though, not unlike a game of Russian roulette. We'd keep talking during the preacher's sermon, never knowing when the bullet of getting a backseat beating had our names on it.

Of course, we all grew up, and many of us kept the habit of going to church. We had even learned to behave by the time we had children of our own. And this is when I learned the lesson my parents and all my friends' parents knew: Never commence to punishing your child during the sermon.

The oldest boy was somewhere between two and three at the time and was bored out of his little mind. To occupy his time, he picked up the Methodist hymnal and began flipping all gazillion pages from hard front cover to hard back cover.

Whap.

Whap.

Whap.

"Stop, baby," I hissed.

Whap.

Whap.

Whap.

It was like the tide, steady and relentless, and also pretty darned loud. I started getting disapproving looks from my fellow congregants.

Whap.

Whap.

Whap.

In desperation, I folded my arms and gave him a pinch, surreptitiously, to get his attention.

Instead, he got mine. Along with the preacher's and everyone else in the congregation that day.

"Mama!" he said in a nice, clear, outside voice. "Quit pinching me!"

The preacher had to pause to get his composure back, shaking while he stifled a laugh, and the choir twittered with muffled laughter until the altar call.

The rest of the week, folks around town would tell me to stop pinching my little boy and laugh. That was the last time he got pinched by me, in church or elsewhere, by the way.

The oldest boy was lucky he was a child of his generation. In the church parking lots of my day, that would have gotten him a walloping of Biblical proportions.

DINNER ON THE GROUNDS

When I was a little girl, I had a clear picture of heaven. It was a church potluck.

We called these "dinner on the grounds" back then, and they were exactly what I would imagine lunch being like in Glory.

Plenty of food made by mamas and mamaws, and plenty of people enjoying each other's company. Laughter, kids running around. Only in the heaven version, there is a never-ending supply of fried chicken drumsticks.

There are a couple of good reasons why we called potlucks dinner on the grounds. One was that this was in north Mississippi, and the noontime meal, if it was heavy, and this most certainly was, was called "dinner." The evening meal would be lighter, and it was called "supper.''A lot of folks don't get this right.

A snack supper, which is something Methodists do from time to time, is in the evening, and let's just say the heavy artillery isn't out. Potlucks are also generally in the evening, and if you are in a Methodist church, there will be at least five Poppyseed Chicken casseroles along with other combinations involving Campbell's soup, sour cream and cheese. A friend of mine, a preacher's daughter, used to call that "goo food," but she could have just added a D to it, because it's all good.

But those of us growing up Baptist had dinners on the grounds, somewhere around noon unless the preacher got on a roll. The "on the grounds'' part came from the fact that lots of churches in that place and time didn't have places for everyone to sit.

The older folks got the folking chairs, our mamas and maybe our daddies did, too, but we kids got "the grounds" or maybe the church steps, which was fine with us. We had to sit at the table all the time for meals, so not having to sit still and behave was glorious.

We'd start these things with preaching in the morning, most likely something on the book of Revelation and going up with the sheep or who knows where with the goats. There would be fifteen stanzas of "Just As I Am'' that would have gone to sixteen if someone didn't walk the center aisle and rededicate his life to Christ.

After that, what we kids referred to as "big church," we'd line up for a loaves and fishes kind of miracle, only instead of fish and bread, there was banana pudding, and perhaps a Coca-Cola-glazed ham thrown in for good measure.

A congregation of one hundred or so somehow brought forth enough casseroles, yard birds, caramel cakes, yeast rolls, ice-box pies and deviled eggs to feed at least twice that number. It wasn't the feeding of 5,000, but we all knew better than to show up without a basket of bread and fish, too.

The back seat of our Riviera had multiple casseroles and desserts, and they made their way, carried oh-so-carefully with dishtowel-covered hands, to the church fellowship hall, where they'd sit through a couple of hours of preaching and teaching and a good thirty minutes of waiting in line and trying not to be impatient. Which is hard when you're a little girl.

By the time food started hitting Styrofoam plates, everything was room temperature and hopefully not a food poisoning risk, but to my knowledge, no one ever keeled over at a dinner on the grounds.

I think it is akin to the belief those people who handle snakes have. Just as they think they are immune to snake venom through the power of God, Baptists and Methodists believe they are immune to the dangers of food that's sat out too long. I am living proof that church potluck food won't kill you.

I was still careful of some foods, though, because Satan is full of trickery, I was told from the pulpit. Why else would there be such things as deviled eggs, and devil's food cake, and deviled ham? And why would they all taste good?

Why would a devil's food cake taste infinitely better than a dry old angel food cake that only people on diets think about eating? And even then, it has to be drowned in strawberries and smothered in Cool Whip just to make it palatable. Nobody has to do anything to make a devil's food cake tempting. It's the work of Lucifer, I tell you.

Knowing that I sure as hell didn't want to go to hell, I avoided these deviilish foods and harbored my doubts about people who'd bring deviled eggs to church. Why not just arrange them in a 666 pattern when you put them out on the buffet? Those eggs weren't to be trusted.

But I confess I did used to love some deviled ham. A deviled ham sandwich on white bread with a cold bottled Coca-Cola was one of life's many pleasures for a girl in the Mississippi of the early 1970s. That was back when I would eat such things, things like Vienna sausages, and not think about what went into them. Only adults do that, thinking about fat and sodium and what part of a hog might be in there, and that takes the devil-iciousness right out of deviled ham.

One of the best parts of dinners on the grounds was that people tended to sit where they wanted. Kids were free to lay claim to a patch of grass, and the adults congregated where they liked, which we didn't care about that much. Adults having conversations over casseroles meant that they were too busy to be getting on to us about whatever we were doing. I don't recall what we could have been doing that was so awful at a dinner on the grounds, but I'm pretty sure we were up to no good at least some of the time.

But the most heavenly part of dinner on the grounds of my childhood, what made me hope that when I crossed over Jordan, a Styrofoam plate would be waiting for me, was, of course, the food.

Sure, it sat out longer than it should have, or would have, had some more folks heeded the altar call so we could have run through "Just As I Am" a couple of times, but dinner on the grounds food would make you wish dinner never ended. The chicken legs were the best, and here, in earthly dinners on the grounds, the chicken plate would be empty for those in the back of the line. Part of my personal belief system is that (a) there is a Heaven, and (b) it has a chicken plate that never runs out of drumsticks.

Then there were the vegetables. Back in the day, we kids only hated veggies like broccoli unless it was swimming in melted Velveeta. Butter beans, corn casserole, pink-eyed purple hulls, green beans out of somebody's garden . . . they were all ridiculously good. Few of us ever slipped our vegetables to the dog under the table.

And there were salads . . . Southern salads, which meant that they were sweet enough to double as a dessert. You could tell it was a salad if it was served on an iceberg lettuce leaf. There were pears with a dollop of mayonnaise and cheese on top, and that was the not-so-sweet variety. There were Jell-O salads of all descriptions, but the best ones had marshmallows in them. There were fruit salads that had, as a main ingredient, a can of fruit pie filling.

And then there was the dessert table. Layer cakes, chess pies, banana pudding and peach cobbler. By the time we reached the dessert table, many of us had already eaten a plate piled high with everything from those deviled eggs to broccoli casserole to hamburger surprise. Dessert was enough to make us full enough to rival Thanksgiving afternoon.

Hymn singing would follow, with everyone retreating home to sleep if they were older than twenty, and read the Sunday funnies if they were younger than twelve. Those in the middle would change from polyester church clothes to jeans and go find out what their friends were doing.

Everybody has their own ideas on the afterlife. Some envision peace and love. Some think of sprouting wings and strumming harps. Not me. If Heaven's not a lot like the dinners on the grounds of my childhood, I will be disappointed.

BEER

Things that adults like tend to be acquired tastes.

For me, beer was one of those. It looks glorious, all amber-colored and golden with a white foam on top, but, as I found out as an under-age teenager, beer takes some getting used to.

Getting to sip a beer after doing what small-town teenagers do when there is nothing to do, which was riding in cars up and down the highway, turning in first at the Sonic, and later at McDonald's, was sort of a thrill. Like what I imagine going to a speakeasy in the 1920s would have been like. Forbidden and charmingly naughty.

It was also nasty-tasting. I imagine that tasting whatever the speakeasies were serving up would have been on the nasty side, too. Two words: Bathtub and gin. What would make anyone want to drink something involving either of those words?

It was all I could do to swallow that first sip of beer. My Tee-totalling mama used to tell me the evils of alcohol, and she was right about it tasting pretty bad.

But apparently it wasn't quite bad enough. As a young mother, it wasn't something I drank, as my kids needed watching with a clear head. It was all I could do to keep up with them sober. Imagine how far off the tracks the train would go if my brain was muddled by alcohol. It is not a pretty thought.

I do remember going to a Chuck E. Cheese party once, back in the brief time when Chuck E. Cheese sold beer. Yes, they did. Baby Daddy was having a beer just to get through the evening, and before long, when he'd get up from the table or look away for a second, I'd drink some, just to take the edge off the bells, whistles and screaming young'uns.

The local Chuck E.'s doesn't sell beer any more. This is a pity, because what they really should be selling is hard liquor and prescription tranquilizers. I have taken my kids to Chuck E.'s and prayed for both in one of those "Jesus, Take the Wheel" moments during dinner.

Beer, for a child of the deep South, has a little naughtiness to it. One of my cousins had a neon beer sign, but it was relegated to the garage at my Aunt Tootsie's house. Why? Because beer was naughty. Preachers said so.

Contrast this to my relations in the midwest. Beer is made from grains. Bread is made from grains. Beer, therefore, is liquid bread to them. Midwesterners don't have the naughtiness in their beer.

This, to me, is unfortunate. If you are going to bother acquiring a taste for something, it should have some naughty to it, just to make it worth the trouble.

I decided I should acquire the taste for beer for social reasons. I had started dating again after twenty-something years, which is enough to make anyone start drinking, and I was going out with friends, too. It was handy to have a go-to beverage that wasn't bourbon strong or iced tea weak. A light beer fit the bill. And what was in my wallet.

I thought it would be easy. Just ask for a Bud Light, or an Amstel Light at a nicer establishment. But, no.

Now beer has gone hipster. It used to be so blue collar. Schlitz. Miller. There were two kinds of beer: regular and light. Tastes great vs. less filling.

Now there are Ballistic Blondes, Arrogant Bastards, Andy Gators, Velvet Roosters and Dead Guys. Hipsters still drink Pabst Blue Ribbons because PBRs are a throwback. And they are still cheap.

At some restaurants, the beer menu is now twice as long than the food menu and far more complex.

Back in the day, people would drink beer to forget about the world, and the way the beer tasted. Now people taste the beer. They swish it around in their mouths and comment on the hops like they themselves are brewmeisters.

If you order a lowly Bud Light at some places, you are looked upon as either having come from under a rock or a neophyte in the hipster beer culture, or just perhaps so hipster that the hipsters haven't even discovered it yet. They don't even know.

PICKY KIDS

I really should be dead about now.

From starvation.

I was one of those picky kids. Maybe you know of a few, or maybe there is one at your house, making your life a complete and utter joy.

They won't eat onions. They don't like anything green. The sight of rare meat, or raw meat about to be cooked, sends them into not being able to think about eating. They have lots of things they won't eat, and usually there are several in a family, only they have different pickinesses, meaning that collectively, they won't eat anything. Making one dinner that everyone gathered around your table loves is like the holy grail, only harder to find.

Often, the picky kid also has a food that is fixated upon. That food is loved more than broccoli is hated, or onions, as the case may be. And that beloved food will be eaten gladly morning, noon and night.

For me, it was peanut butter sandwiches. I am no longer picky, but I still love a good PB sandwich, minus the J. For my oldest Dear Son, it was scrambled eggs. He could tear through a dozen eggs faster than a fox in the hen house.

I told the pediatrician about this. Eating nothing but scrambled eggs can't be healthy, I thought. Remember, God does have a sense of humor, so grown picky children get to raise picky offspring.

I was worried about him starving, much like the grown-ups worried about me.

"Is he lethargic?" she asked.

"Are you kidding?"

This kid was into fifteen things simultaneously.

"Then keep the scrambled eggs coming," she said.

And sure enough, the little boy who hated green things grew up to be a man who hates green things. He will still put away some scrambled eggs, though.

Picky kids have it easier now. Back in the day, pickiness was seen as something to be driven out of a child like that demon in Linda Blair. Being possessed by a hatred of the food in front of you was seen as awful, dreadful behavior. Maybe being picky was not as bad as acting up in church, and certainly not as bad as levitating and having your head spin around like in *The Exorcist*, but pickiness was its own form of bad.

In the deep South of the early 1970s, being picky was not simply disliking onions or cornbread dressing or turnip greens. It was like you were spitting on the person who cooked them. It didn't matter that you would hate those things no matter who cooked them or how they were cooked, it was a slap-you-in-the-face insult.

Not only that, but being picky was also seen as a sign of disrespect to the person who earned the money to buy the food. So you were now disrespecting mama and daddy.

But let's add another layer to the evilness of hating onions or green things or whatever. It was also seen as somehow being arrogant enough to think you somehow lived at Joe's Bar and Grill and could issue short orders.

One more layer: The Depression. Being picky in front of a grown-up who grew up in the Great Depression is just heresy. It was an afront to all that was good and right about the world.

And let's not forget the cherry on top of this pickiness sundae, the starving children in China. I was told this multiple times in multiple places.

"Children are starving in China."

I never understood why that related to me not liking onions at the time. How would me eating those onions put food on the plates of Chinese children? It would have made sense for us to just send them my onions. Or to forgo buying onions and instead take our onion savings and offer it up to Christ for a Starving Children of China fund.

No, the logic was that I should say, "Ha ha, starving kids in China. I eat every danged thing in front of me, because I am in America, commies."

The whole thing seems to have backfired, though. Parents when I was an ankle-biter on up were worried about us all being too skinny.

"What do you live on?" I would get asked.

I would be thinking, "Peanut butter sandwiches. Duh," but I knew better than to utter something like that. Saying "duh" to an adult happens all the time now, but back then, it would have resulted in one of those time-travel wallopings, the kind preceded by the warning that you were about to be knocked into next week.

But I digress. The pendulum of worry over the pickiness and skinniness of kids back in the day has swung over into us all worrying about the obesity of kids now. Man, if those starving children in China could see us all now. Eating enough to have Type 2 diabetes at a young age. Ha!

But guess what? Kids are still picky.

In a news report, a child criticized a healthy school lunch, one promoted by the White House, as tasting like vomit. While I now love cornbread dressing, back in the day, I totally thought cornbread dressing tasted like vomit, but I was never crazy enough to say that, let alone to a news reporter. If I had, I would be unable to sit to this day.

Today's kids have more mouth, but not enough veggies or love for them. Plus in some places, it's easier and cheaper to find some honey buns than it is to find something grown out of the ground.

And it's harder to get a meal on the table, am I right, mamas? Dinner was always a couple of veggies, meat, rolls, maybe salad and dessert when I was growing up, but our mamas, by and large, were not working for a paycheck. Or if they did, it wasn't an all-day gig. There was time and energy to get a sit-down dinner on.

We have nights at our house when I get dinner on, much in the fashion that my own mama did, and then there are nights when all the wheels come off at work and it is all I could do to limp home and shower off the stench of failure. And a few nights in between on the scale of pretty good to "Jesus, take the wheel."

On those nights when the needle swings toward Jesus, we get pizza. And my children rise up and call me blessed.

They even play me. Like a cheap Nintendo 64 at a yard sale marked-down table.

"Hi, Mom," they say. "How was work?"

"Rough," I say.

"Aww, Mom, you should relax. You don't have to cook tonight. We could get pizza. We love you, Mama."

It works every time.

Of course, if we order a pizza, it can't have onions. Or peppers. Or black olives. The kids are picky about those things.

ICE CREAM

The answer to world peace is ice cream.

It can solve just about all problems, except the issue of fitting into skinny jeans. Why?

Because it is impossible to harbor anger, sadness or any negative thoughts or feelings while eating ice cream.

Go ahead and try it. I'll wait.

Back in the day, every summer there was ice cream, and while folks could either go to the Big Star to pick up a half gallon or drive into Columbus to the Baskin-Robbins, quite a few people still made homemade ice cream. Just about every summer, during revival week at church, there was an ice cream social, and volunteers were asked to do their "loaves and fishes" part and offer up to Jesus a batch of French vanilla or butter pecan.

Miracles involving feeding a crowd with ice cream are pretty sweet, after all. I figure Jesus was partial to fish since he hung around with a few fishermen, but anything as good as ice cream has to be blessed.

Our ice cream maker was a hand-cranked one, and I was just young and hyper enough to think turning the crank was great fun. I would beg to do it, and I would turn and turn and turn until there was no feeling in my arm. Daddy would usually take over then.

I had those good memories of making ice cream with mama and daddy, and good memories of eating ice cream, so we went out and bought an ice cream maker so the Dear Sons and the Dear Daughter would have those good memories, too.

There is one major difference between a kid-powered ice cream maker and an electric one. I don't remember a hand-cranked ice cream maker being loud enough to wake the dead. The electric one we bought was.

Dear Lord. We tried having it in the house but it ran us crazy within about five minutes. So then I took it to the driveway and let it irritate the neighbors a while. A chainsaw cutting down a redwood made out of steel would have been less noisy. Let's phrase it as an SAT question: Good is to ice cream as noise is to an electric ice cream maker.

We used it exactly one time. Nothing tastes good enough to be worth that racket.

Not even homemade ice cream.

The electric ice cream maker wound up at the Salvation Army, and we continued buying our ice cream from the store.

Mint chocolate chip got me through finishing a master's degree, one bowl at a time. Nothing will make you write a paper for a business class faster than having a bowl of ice cream as the carrot at the end of the stick.

My daddy's favorite was chocolate. Butter pecan will lure the Gentleman Friend in after an evening out.

It's the weirdo flavors for the Dear Daughter. Bubble gum. Cotton Candy. Red Velvet cake. If it is neopolitan or strawberry or cookies and cream, she'd not that interested. I didn't say not interested, because she'll still eat it.

Since every family is a mixed bag, her brother loves vanilla with no toppings. He is a purist.

Another thing about ice cream is that you can eat a three course meal including an appetizer and still have room for ice cream. It's because it doesn't take up space. It just melts into a heavenly fluid that fills any nooks and crannies in the belly.

So that means you can always find room for some ice cream.

Now they have smoothies and frozen yogurt, which is like ice cream without the guilt. Like I had any guilt. For me, those just give me the feeling not of less guilt but more healthiness. I am drinking a fruit smoothie so I am healthier than thou.

But as much as I enjoy a frappe, smoothie or a frozen California Tart frozen yogurt with strawberries and kiwi, it's not ice cream. It's close but no cigar. Not that I like cigars, because they don't smell like they would taste anything close to ice cream.

Another time I decided to be all healthier than thou, I bought sugar-free ice cream that was also low fat. It's not that I didn't eat the stuff, because I did, but if I am referring to it as "stuff," then it is nowhere near as good as real ice cream. By real, I mean that it is made with sugar and something richer than skim milk.

Some things are just worth it. They're worth the cost, they're worth the calories or the time on the treadmill or the larger size of blue jeans.

Ice cream is one of those things. World peace is, too, but it's just a byproduct.

THE BEAR AND THE CAT

This is a story about love, loss and a head getting detached.

Few things are loved as hard as Teddy bears. They are often our first friends and our best ones. They never tell secrets, repeat gossip or talk behind anyone's back. They are the perfect sidekicks as they never say no to exploring or swashbuckling. Teddy bears are brave.

In the case of my middle son's Bear, named The Bear, few animals had the adventures he had. His boy would set out, wearing a pretend fire fighter's helmet and Fisher-Price binoculars around his neck, his trusty bear from Grandma in his hand, and you just knew they were off to do great things.

The Bear never told his tales, and neither did his boy. Perhaps they were too dangerous and adventuresome to repeat. Maybe the two were spies, and speaking would endanger national security, or given the boy's gear, they might have been out spotting forest fires and putting them out.

The Bear would become filthy at times, but he would have to be spirited away from his boy in the dead of night for a rendezvous with the washing machine, then tumble-dried and tucked back in, or else the boy would howl. The Bear never spoke of these adventures either, but one could tell they were harrowing times, even if he did see a bear on the bottle of fabric softener.

The Bear would go on to get dirty on new adventures, and if the boy noticed his bear was fluffy and smelled like spring rain, he never spoke of it and never held it against The Bear. He was just happy to have his friend each day, a companion for life's journey.

Cats can be loved like that, too.

The youngest son, as an infant, was given a soft, blue stuffed cat. If the cat was a bear, he'd have been a Teddy bear, but he was a cat. He was the size of my son when the gift was received, but the Cat's boy quickly outgrew him.

They went hand in paw everywhere, the youngest boy and Cat. Like The Bear, Cat was aptly named. And like Bear, Cat craved adventure. He loved to climb trees, like cats and little boys do. He and the youngest boy were peas in a pod, always wanting to explore and always wanting the other around. When you're out having adventures, you need someone to have your back when pirates are around.

But the greatest nemesis to Bear wasn't any old buccaneer. It was an older brother.

Bear's boy had one of those, and because Bear was so beloved, because having Bear away would make the boy go into fits, the older brother would kidnap Bear. The Bear's boy would wail and then take the extreme step of "telling Mom."

This went on from time to time until one day the boys, let's call them Cain and Abel, were in a tug-of-war with Bear as the rope. Oldest was trying to snatch away Bear, with youngest hanging on, white-knuckled, to his friend.

Something had to give. It was Bear's head.

It came right off, in perhaps the wildest adventure Bear had seen. Let's face it, if your head comes off as a result, you've had an adventure.

"Telling mom" happened momentarily, and the oldest got to sit in the time-out chair and think about things while the The Bear's best friend sat sniffling, watching The Bear's head get reattached one stitch at a time. Mom could do anything if she knew how to reattach heads.

Bear, having lost his head and then having the dangerous head-reattachment surgery, went on to have more adventures until one day his boy got older. He went off to school, relegating The Bear to the task of guarding his room. He now sits in semi-retirement in the room of Mom, the head reattacher.

Cat also had a mortal enemy, one called a little sister. She absconded with Cat and tortured him by taking him to tea parties and rocking him like a baby. The Cat's boy just knew that Cat hated that. She would all but put him in a dress.

One day, though, Cat took off on perhaps his greatest adventure. Cat's boy, the little sister and Bear's head re-attacher were among the group dressed as shepherds riding atop the Madison United Methodist Christmas float that year. Cat came along, and Cat's boy, perhaps thinking about what baby Jesus would do, let the little sister hold Cat.

She promised to hold onto his paw, but somewhere along the parade route, Cat went flying. He was gone. The head re-attacher tried in vain to be a cat finder, retracing the route over and over again.

Cat's boy was broken-hearted. The head re-attacher took him to pick out another stuffed friend, but you can't just buy those off the shelf. He picked one, but it wasn't the same. The stuffed Pokemon character didn't go on adventures like Cat did. He just sat on the bed and looked straight ahead.

We like to think that Cat 's work with the boy was done, and it was true that the boy was growing up. He wouldn't be able to take Cat to school, and school, big school, kindergarten, wasn't far off. Maybe someone else needed to have some adventures. Maybe, since we were all thinking about baby Jesus that day, it was a God thing. Maybe Cat went where he was called.

GUITAR MAN

There comes a time in all children's lives when they want guitars.

It is because guitars make people look cool. Oh, sure, later those who are serious about playing will fall in love with the music and pour themselves into learning how to play well, but in the beginning, it is about the coolness.

Ever wonder why supermodels date rock stars? It is because the guitars make whoever is holding them look super cool and awesome.

Don't believe me? Young men, go walk around your nearest shopping mall or watering hole holding a six-string with humbuckers. You will immediately notice that girls who otherwise would not look at you will actually not mind being seen with you or even want to be on your non-guitar-holding arm.

If you give them your phone number, they will ring it off the hook.

It happened to us.

Second Dear Son hit his guitar phase.

I was thinking, "OK, this will not last. Let's get him the cheapest guitar going." I think it came from Walmart or a pawn shop. I honestly don't remember the store because I scoured the area for a deal. Again, if I thought it would be something that would last, I'd have put some buckeroos behind it. As if I had many of those, but you get the concept.

He dug in, though.

One summer, this child went to the library and checked out a *Guitar for Dummies* book. He kept renewing it all summer. Baby Daddy knew a few chords and taught him those, but the rest Second Dear Son did on his own. Before long, he was creating raw spots on his fingers from playing guitar and breaking them open playing baseball.

He then gave up baseball.

By eighth grade, he played guitar for a friend's school choir concert solo. The middle school groupies started calling not long after.

I couldn't go to a store, it seemed, without a middle school girl asking me if my son was with me or how he was doing or to call her.

In those early days of social media, I read a comment from some little fan girl who posted that he was a "sexy beast." I nearly hurt myself laughing. I am sorry, eighth-graders, but no one your age is a sexy beast. Brad Pitt would have been geeky and awkward in eighth grade.

Unless he was holding a guitar, that is.

Awkward young teen plus guitar equals sexy beast.

As he kept playing, it became time to invest in some lessons, too, and before long, the electric guitar, the shredding that would scare off the Jehovah's Witnesses on Saturday mornings and add to the rocking of the youth praise band on Sunday nights, gave way to classical guitar.

And incredible beauty.

There were recitals, competitions and concertos, not to mention my quest to find someone who would make petits fours with maroon music notes on them for his senior recital at Mississippi State.

He's now a graduate student in guitar performance at the University of Memphis, and it's now about the substance. He plays gigs here and there and the occasional wedding, and he works tirelessly to improve his artistry.

And he still looks pretty cool holding a guitar.

HIDING CATS

There are irresistable forces in this world.

Little girls and kittens are two of them.

Try saying no to a little girl holding a kitten. It can't be done. The word will not leave your lips.

There were kittens in our neighborhood, a whole litter of them, a squirming box full of them just down the street, and two of them escaped, sauntering past our front yard. For my daughter, about six at the time, this was a miracle, better than

117

a winning lottery ticket, and while not quite as cool as discovering a unicorn, it was right up there.

Dodging the view of her older brother, she scooped them up and carried them to her brother's closet. Which, in hind sight, was pretty smart. Had she gotten into trouble, she could always claim they were his. After all, they were in his closet.

A spare laundry basket, a few towels and a blanket became a bed for the pair, one black with white paws and one a gray tabby. So far, so good, she had to be thinking.

In the kitchen, she poured a large glass of milk.

"Baby, I love seeing you pick something healthy to drink," I said while cooking dinner.

This should have tipped me off. When will a 6-year-old pass up a bottle of soda for the milk jug? When she's hiding kittens, that's when.

But, full of milk and on a fluffy homemade bed, the little cats weren't making a sound. Her brother was sleeping, undisturbed by mews, until morning.

The next day, a Saturday, the plan was still working. The little girl was hanging out with me while breakfast was cooking when her brother, about 8, woke up screaming.

"Mom! There's something ALIVE in my closet!"

Those are words no mother wants to hear. I'm thinking, "Please don't be a raccoon, please don't be a raccoon."

We went running upstairs, and sure enough, there were cries coming from behind the closet door.

"Those sound like kittens!''I said. "Do either of you know anything about kittens being in the closet?''

"Mom, if I knew about any kittens, why would I be screaming?'' the boy asked, and he had a point.

The kitten rescuer pleaded innocent long past the point of being figured out. It wasn't until she knew she'd get to keep a kitten if her neighbors approved, until she knew she wasn't in trouble, that she 'fessed up. Six-year-old girls are like that.

The little gray tabby is now about seven years old, and her rescuer has grown up, too. The girl has a soft spot in her heart for cats, still, and I have a soft spot in mine for her.

Cats, by the way, are like potato chips … it's hard to have just one of them. People realize this when they have kittens to give away. They say, "But you already have cats!'' when you tell them no.

It is hard to get someone to take the first "starter cat,'' but then once you own a litter box, the world tries to turn you into a crazy cat lady one kitten at a time.

My oldest Dear Son's friend Ben had a cat who became a mama, and he wanted one of the kittens. He picked an adorable orange and white male who wanted to rip the world a new one with his tiny claws. We went from calling him Cat Scratch Fever to Ted Nugent. When the oldest moved off and left the nest, he took Ted with him. I refer to him as my grandkitty.

Then we gained another cat when Honey, a little yellow kitten, was crying outside *The Clarion-*

Ledger building in downtown Jackson. It was a cold December, and I could hear her all the way from my office on the second floor. Several of us took to leaving food out, hoping we could get this tiny motherless cat to come out of hiding. Greta, who's something of a cat whisperer, lured her into a cage, and the email went out.

The cat couldn't live inside the newspaper building, and someone was going to have to step up or she'd have to get released. It was supposed to dip to 18 degrees that night. I knew about the last thing I needed was another mouth to feed, but Christmas was coming. I couldn't live with a dead cat on my conscience, so off I went to get the cat. The Dear Daughter was bouncing with excitement on the backseat over the thought of having another kitten.

All these kittens tended to coincide with milestones for my children. Just about the time we would get a cat, someone would graduate from something and/or move off to college.

"You know, Mom, you can't replace us with cats," the second Dear Son said to me one day about this coincidence,

"Cats are less expensive," I countered. Sometimes I think they mind better.

Another day, I was musing about being alone after the kids all moved out.

This same son said, "But Mom, you won't be alone. You have the cats!"

BARBIES

My cousins had the best Barbies. They were teenagers when I was a little girl, so the Barbies they would take out to humor me were the Barbies of the early 1960s.

They had stiff legs, molded eyelashes that were thick and painted black and eyes that were large and glancing sideways the way Audrey Hepburn did in "Breakfast at Tiffany's." I thought they were, style wise, miles beyond the Barbies of my day, which had bendable joints, sun-bleached stick-straight hair and pre-cancerous tans.

As long as the classic Barbies were standing, they looked elegant. Sitting down with their legs stuck straight out, not so much, but standing was a different story. Jackie Kennedy elegant. Grace Kelly elegant.

"Do you want to play Barbies?"

It was the best five words in the world. The answer was always yes.

I remember us girls bringing Barbies to school and playing with them on the playground at recess. Keeping them in our desks and not peeking at them was next to impossible, though.

Sometimes there were Barbie weddings, and we'd pick dandelions for bouquets, and the procession would be at the sandbox or, if on the weekend, in someone's front yard.

After the vows, Barbie and Ken would ride off to marital bliss in a plastic car, or a shoebox. Either one would work.

Then there were fashion shows, because Barbie's job, other than renewing her vows with Ken hundreds of times, was being a fashion model.

In northeast Mississippi of the early 1970s, stores didn't have a great selection of Barbie clothes, but we had mamas who knew how to sew. There were Barbie clothing patterns, and sometimes the scraps from a little girl's dress would be turned into a Barbie frock. At McClure's Furniture, there were handmade Barbie dresses for sale, each in a little plastic sandwich bag. I had a gold one made from fabric that looked like it might have been remnants from curtains. To me, it might as well have been gold brocade. I loved it.

We'd bounce-step our Barbies down the pretend runway, narrating along the way about the chiffon cascading from her evening gown. I doubt any of our Barbie clothes were actually chiffon, but it sounded good.

"Barbie is modeling a chiffon gown with sparkles and flowers straight from Paris, France."

Paris also made it sound good, and everything had sparkles and flowers.

This was in the days of soft drinks in glass bottles. Not only does Coca-Cola taste best in a glass bottle, but there was a side benefit to those bottles for us girls. There were bottle caps. Some kids might have turned those into checkers pieces, but for us, bottle caps were Barbie plates. Our Barbies each had a service for eight of Grape Nehi, Yoo-Hoo or Orange Crush.

Another cousin of mine had G.I. Joes, but he did not want his soldiers fraternizing with Barbie, Skipper and Midge.

We loved our Barbies, and I couldn't understand why my teenage cousins would put theirs away.

Why would you not play with your Barbies forever? I never wondered this about my mama or her friends, many of whom were my friends' mamas because they had their hands full dealing with us and getting supper on the table for us and our daddies. But my cousins who had the elegant stiff-legged Barbies? There was no good reason for them not to play with their Barbies after high school let out or, in the case of one, before sorority meetings at Mississippi State.

Until one day, I looked at my Barbies and felt a little embarrassed to be playing with them. The golden brocade evening gown was curtain remnants and not covered with sparkles and flowers. Her gown was from West Point, Mississippi, not Paris, France. I had somehow crossed over from believing in make-believe and magic to realism.

It's called growing up. Everyone does it, but it's a little overrated.

My Barbies went away, hanging out in cardboard boxes instead of my made-up fashion show runways and marriage chapels. After a while, they either went to a yard sale or the landfill during a move. They deserved a better fate.

Then I went on to be my daughter's mama. She had her Barbies and loved them. She'd take off with her brother's G.I. Joe landing craft and let Barbie and her friend Hannah Montana go on a boat ride in the bathtub, sparking World War III once this was discovered. Those Barbies would wind up naked when the teenage boys in the house were around, causing no small amount of horror once she discovered the dressed Barbies she left in the living room were starkers.

Occasionally I would have to become a Barbie doctor and pop heads back on while she sniffled and dried her tears. I could reattach heads, making me somewhat of a miracle worker in the plastic fashion doll community, but I couldn't do much to fix Barbie haircuts other than finding a small hat or a scrap of fabric for a scarf. Barbie could do just about anything but grow hair.

In my daughter's world, Barbie had hit records, starred in movies and jetsetted around wherever she wanted to go. I am sure her gowns also had sparkles and flowers from Paris, France. Until one day, my girl went out to play without a Barbie in her right hand. I knew my youngest was growing up.

Which all little girls do. It's a shame that growing up means some of life's magic gets packed up and put away. We should all choose to keep the chiffon cascading from our gowns, even if we're wearing jeans and a T-shirt.

RUNNING

I used to be the last kid picked.

Team captains would argue over who had to take me into their kickball fold. Klutziness and lack of speed could turn a child into a playground pariah and did.

I'd wish for some redeeming quality and tried, but in the end, I was still that last kid running what seemed like a mile behind everyone else. Even the good-natured ribbing hurt.

Later, the physical education coaches had us running. Stopping resulted in getting screamed at, and making a trip to the water fountain was a sign of weakness. Slacking might get you extra laps. Running wasn't fun. It was punishment.

So running? Not necessarily high on my list of things to do for quite some time. I associated it with emotional and physical pain, and who in her right mind would sign up for that?

Well, I would, eventually.

Years ago, non-runner me decided to help a friend by volunteering to register runners in his 5K fundraiser and hand out water. My two youngest were in tow and begged to run in the fun run afterward, so I signed them up. While I was watching them, cheering for them from the sidewalk, I saw friends of mine running alongside their kids.

Why am I not doing that? I thought.

Some of these moms and dads had just run a little over three miles and were taking another mile on. This, to me, seemed incredible. But they looked happy, and their kids looked happy, so why was I missing out on this?

I went out and bought the best pair of running shoes I had ever owned, and also the most expensive pair of shoes I had ever worn. I then went out and ran hard, gasping for air before I reached the end of the block.

Running sucks, I thought.

But I had invested in the pricey shoes, and I can't stand to spend money without getting some value from it. So I kept on, feeling like a failure if I walked or stopped and berating myself for a lack of anything resembling speed.

I quit a few times. Hard to imagine why, with the physical and mental pain double whammy going on. But those sparkly blue Adidas were sitting in the closet.

"Annie," they'd say. "You wasted money on us."

These taunting shoes were just asking to be worn out.

Running a 5K became a bucket list item for me, and I rationalized that if I joined a class, I would have to follow through. Or be the class wimp, and that was not about to happen. I quit being a wimp when I became a mama. Running is not as painful as childbirth, even with an epidural, and as any mama will tell you, childbirth is the easiest part of raising babies.

I learned quite a few things about running and life metaphors in that class and on the city's trails and sidewalks since. Here are ten of them:

1. **Pace yourself.** Life, like most runs, is not a sprint. Patience and persistence pay off in every area of life, and reaching the goals you set count no matter your speed. A mile is a mile, whether you run it in six minutes or sixteen, so enjoy everything, life or a run, at your own pace.

2. **Perfection isn't required.** You don't have to be the fastest one, and you don't have to

126

look like a bronze goddess when you cross the finish line. Feeling like you have to be perfect is a sure-fire way to feel like a failure.

3. **Be your kids' role model.** Letting kids see you sweat and work for a goal, then accomplish it and surpass it, leads them to say, "Well, if my mama can do that, then I can do …" Fill in the blank with whatever pie-in-the-sky goal they've got. You hit your goals, and they'll hit theirs.

4. **Wear awesome shoes**.

5. **Listen to the cheers, but don't take it too seriously.** Hearing "Mom, you rock" yelled from the lips of your child is guaranteed to add bounce to your steps, in a 5K or in life. Just know that your child may also do as mine did when I earned my first medal, for coming in third in my age group. "Wow, Mom," he said, "So only two other people in your age group showed up?" Kids will always keep your ego in check.

6. **Falling down is still moving forward.** So is walking. Just keep going.

7. **Consistency defines you.** It's not life's little slip-ups that trip you up, but the things you do every day. Do things that are positive for your life every day, physically, mentally, spiritually and emotionally, and you will see positive change.

8. **Take time for yourself.** Go for a run, or read a book, paint your toenails or just drink a glass of tea while sitting in the back yard.

If you can't take time to do something for yourself that renews you and brings you happiness, then you will bring less to those you love. I tried not doing this, and trust me, I am right.

9. **Sometimes you run with the pack, and sometimes you are the lone wolf.** Running with friends is great fun and can make your steps faster, but a solitary run can give you time to think and feel. In life, as in running, there are times when you go with the crowd and times when you go it alone.

10. **Get spiritual.** Running has given me the uninterrupted time to pray more deeply and for things that I'd have never considered otherwise. When the psalmist writes of thirsting for God, runners get that. Being thirsty and out of breath made me thankful for the oft-taken-for-granted things such as water and air. "Thank you, God, for liquids," said every runner, even atheist ones.

I signed up for the 5K, and the fear I had of someone giggling at the thought of me running in public turned out to be completely unfounded. As was my fear of being the last one across the finish line. But even if that happens, and it may, as a runner friend of mine wailed in a race, "Hurry, the walkers are gaining on us," no one who tries ever comes in last.

I'm no longer the last kid picked, and you don't have to be either. All that's required to avoid that distinction is making sure you pick yourself first.

VACATION BIBLE SCHOOL

I can't eat store-brand cookies and drink grape Kool-aid without thinking of Jesus.

It's because of Vacation Bible School. We went every summer. Like clockwork. If we were not making little Play-Doh Ten Commandments tablets and singing songs to remember the books of the Bible, our little souls might be heading straight for hell.

Some kids got enrolled in a summer's worth of Vacation Bible School, because every church held one. If a mama timed it right, a child could go to a few Baptist Vacation Bible Schools, a Methodist one, maybe even Presbyterian and Episcopalian. By the end of the summer, mom's gotten a little R&R and junior is ready to receive his divinity degree.

Growing up Baptist, I got a big dose of VBS. We did it old school, because, well, there was no "new school" back then. Now, there are large-church VBSes that come complete with a praise band Christian rock concert and light show and a curriculum that can compete with kids' secular interests. They have everything but pyrotechnics these days.

There was a curriculum this year about rollercoasters. I do get that life has its ups and downs, but there's something that makes me giggle about putting Jesus on a rollercoaster. I know, I know. I am heading straight for H-E-double hockey sticks.

No, our Bible School back in the day didn't have a curriculum about rollercoasters, and other than a poster of Jesus from the Baptist publishing house, there were no special decorations. Our curriculum was the King James Bible. Hardbacked.

No flippy-flopping Bibles for us. We had hardbacked Bibles to make sword drill that much harder.

Sword drill was a key part of Vacation Bible School of the early 1970s in small town Mississippi. For the uninitiated, the teacher would say, "Phillippians 4:13," for example.

Then a flurry of page-turning would ensue, and the future pastor of the class would step forward confidently and reply, "I can do all things through Christ which strengtheneth me." And the page would be checked to make sure the winning swordsman looked up the verse and was not just spouting off a memory verse. Because cheating on sword drill would be the exit from the straight and narrow to the on-ramp of Hades Boulevard.

There was an opening service each morning, but back in the day, there was no praise band. We would pledge allegiance to the Christian flag and the American flag, and the boys would practice ushering by passing the plates. Girls at that time got to practice sitting down and keeping quiet.

Then there were backyard Bible Schools. Because you might not get enough Jesus during regular Bible School. Teenagers would hold them, and once, when I was old enough to help, we had communion with saltines and grape Kool-Aid. The grape Kool-Aid would have also been a good aide in acting out Jesus turning the water into wine at the marriage at Cana. I wish we'd have thought of that, because turning water into Kool-Aid is easier than trying to bring Lazarus back to life or walking on water.

There were kickball games back then, and of course, the store brand cookies and Kool-Aid, which was served up in little cups that we'd gulp down in two seconds. Playing kickball in 11 a.m. north Mississippi heat will bring thoughts of hell's temperature to mind. You really, really do not want to go there.

None of us did.

And so we all bought a little fire insurance.

Most of us Baptist kids, during one summer or another, asked Jesus to be our personal Lord and savior. We got prayed up, and then, following the preacher, who was wearing a white robe and waders, we were each dunked. I remember taking a huge breath just in case the preacher thought I could hold my breath longer than I really could. Drowning during a dunking would be the ticket straight to Heaven and perhaps having a missions offering named in your honor.

But it was a Baptism, not a dunking at the local swimming pool. We took it seriously. Jesus had said to let the little children come to him, so we did.

That's not to say we weren't rotten a good bit of our growing-up years, or that we didn't make mistakes or stray away and sleep in on Sundays for years at a time. Because most of us except for that kid who won at sword drill all the time did those things and more.

The lessons taught to us by our beehived mothers in a hot church, though, stuck. Forgiveness, love, faith, loyalty, doing the right thing even though the thought of the consequences was what kept us from the evil we didn't do . . . these were all lessons washed down with sugar water dyed purple on hot summer mornings.

SKINNED KNEES

I believe I went through most of my young life with scraped knees. I was probably a teenager before I had scabless legs.

Most of us were covered with bumps and skinned spots. If we don't each have a scar or two with a story to tell about them, then our childhoods were wasted.

Back when we mamas and mee-maws were little girls, skinned knees were treated with something called "Monkey Blood." It was reddish brown and was dabbed on with a fuzz ball dangled into the Monkey Blood bottle with what looked like a piece of coathanger wire,

Having your skinned knee treated with Monkey Blood was like medieval torture. Really, all treatments for skinned knees used to be worse than the original skinning. The smart ones among us would bottle up any crying over getting the skinned knee because then the Monkey Blood would come out. Just brushing off the knee and walking it off was the wise move.

And there was alcohol. The rubbing kind. Childbirth is not as bad as having alcohol dabbed or poured onto a skinned knee. It is at the "stepping on a Lego at night" level of pain. The treatment was far worse than the injury.

I remember being a total pansy when it came to skinned knees, sniffling as a Band-Aid was put on. Those were deceptive, soothing when they went on but back to medieval torture when it was time to rip those off. Why do women endure bikini waxing? Because they figure nothing could possibly be worse than having a Band-Aid ripped off a knee that was skinned the day before.

You'd think, with skinned knees and their treatment being a one-two punch of awfulness, that we'd watch what we were doing, but we didn't, ever, and we were girls. Boys were worse. I remember boys being covered with mud and scabs most of the time. It is a wonder we survived childhood to worry over our own wild children.

The reason we kept getting skinned was because the risk of it was worth the fun. Risk is like that. Risky but fun.

Climbing trees is fun. Falling out of them is not, but you don't fall out of the mimosa tree every day. For every skinned knee kind of day you have, you have fifteen all-climbing no-Monkey Blood days. Like Clint Eastwood said, do you feel lucky? And we did, of course, right up to the moment of skin hitting ground.

Getting skinned as a child was bad, but getting skinned as an adult is, in some ways, worse. The fall hurts more, but no one bigger than you holds you down and paints you with Monkey Blood

I got a good skinning during a holiday 5K run a year or so ago. It was at night, and even though most people had Christmas lights on, some tree-hugging Scrooges didn't. Go ahead, save some pandas and a little money on your electric bill, but the pothole in front of your house that was cloaked in your anti-Christmas darkness got me.

Nothing impresses other runners like hitting a pothole and landing spread-eagle on the pavement while screaming all the way down. It was pretty awesome, I must admit.

I managed to scrape a knee and both palms. They stung even after I dug the gravel out of them. I immediately had a new-found respect for children who brave skinned knees, and I was grateful that my yoga pants didn't tear. Knees heal, but not so yoga pants.

It hurt bad enough to cry, but nobody wants to see a woman in her 40s crying at a 5K. I was telling those tears to get back in those ducts with a few curse words that I hope stayed in my head and didn't exit through my mouth.

I was about a mile off from the finish line. It was too dark to see much of the damage, so I decided to just run the rest of the race and not be wimpy. After you've gone a couple of miles, you're in no mood to quit. So I ran a slower than normal 5K, but no one tried to put Monkey Blood on me. Instead, they handed me a beer at the finish line, and that took the sting out considerably.

Running in the dark while dressed like Mrs. Claus is tree-climbing risky, but it was fun right up until the skin hit the pavement. It was kind of fun after getting some grown-up boo-boos because then I was "that girl who fell down but ran the rest of the way." I felt sort of like a bad-ass, holding my can of beer with bleeding hands. Plus everyone who was in earshot of me was either as slow as I was or slower.

No one ever gets skinned while sitting on the sofa, but sitting on the sofa is overrated. Trees have to be climbed, races have to be run, chances have to be taken, and sometimes knees have to get skinned in the process.

Metaphorically speaking, mamas take all kinds of risks, starting with bringing a child into the world. It only gets more risky from there. Sometimes we get skinned, and sometimes our babies do, which hurts us more than it hurts them. I used to hear that when I was painted with Monkey Blood, and figured at the time that the grown-ups in my life were all liars, but when you have children of your own, you really do hurt when they do. Not Monkey Blood bad, but bad enough.

But the risks are worth it, whether you're a kid or a midlifer who thinks she's a kid. The benefits of living a full life far outweigh sitting on the sofa.

Take the risks worth taking, and find something less painful than Monkey Blood. And for those over twenty-one, a cold beer can take the sting out of being skinned considerably.

COME TO PASS

A summer ago, our house was full.

Everyone was home. The oldest son graduated from Southern Miss and was living at home and working. His brother had graduated from Mississippi State and was home the summer before grad school. The younger siblings were home while school was out. Plus there were friends over.

The washing machine never stopped, and there were never enough dishes or glasses. The house wasn't neat for more than fifteen minutes. Clean towels were a commodity. When everyone was home and watching TV or otherwise hanging out in the living room, chairs from the dining room had to be carried in.

It was glorious.

Sure, the house was a mess, but it was a mess made by people I love. If running out of glasses and drying off with a bed sheet because all the towels were gone when I stepped out of the shower is a sign of all my sweet babies being home, then I could tolerate it, if not love it all the time.

But that August, the middle son moved to Memphis. About two months later, his older brother was packing up to move to Missouri after being transferred for a promotion. When older children move for work, you might get a little vacation time, but the summer breaks are gone.

This summer, I had the older kids home for about a week each, but most of the time there were the three of us here. But I have a teen and a tween still at home. I am using the words "at home" loosely, as any mama with kids that age knows they are gone for any number of good reasons. There's church youth groups and sports teams and friends to see.

At least two weeks of this summer, it's just me and the Dear Daughter. And while I love that girl like I love breathing, it is taking some adjustment for me to accept the house going from always full to nearly empty in a short twelve months.

Mamas of small children, I know you are thinking that they will never grow up. It may seem like you will never get your kids out of diapers, or out of day care or school or fill in the blank, but like the Good Book says, things come to pass. Phases come, and they pass. Little in life stays the same for long, and that is especially true for children.

I remember going to First United Methodist in West Point when the boys were young, and sweet senior members of the congregation would comment on how they were growing like weeds.

"You blink, and they'll be grown," they'd say.

I'd smile and laugh and thank them, thinking these were merely things polite people say. But these were more than just pleasantries. These were warnings.

One day, your children will grow up.

I cried last fall when my youngest was starting middle school. She looks more like a teenage girl and a lot less like the ponytailed little thing who used to bounce around the house dressed like a Disney princess, a Barbie in each hand.

137

Mothers of sons, I will warn you that they will grow up to shave and drive cars. They one day will be able to buy a beer legally. They will probably be taller than you are.

The little boys they used to be, if not gone completely, are hidden beneath the exterior of young men. It is akin to the question of whether a glass is half full or heading toward empty: I can think about how much I miss the child or that I have this great young adult now. Sometimes I think both at the same time, loving the young adult but missing that kid.

The lesson in life from all this, going from a summer of a full house to a summer of three of a kind and sometimes a pair, is that life is to be enjoyed in the moment. Summers, full houses and phases of life come to pass.

Change is happening constantly, even if you don't always see it happening. If you spend your children's teen and young adult years missing the kids they once were, then you miss out on something that won't come around again.

It is like shutting your eyes on life's rollercoaster. While I do shut my eyes tightly on any scary fair ride I might dare to hop on, I try not to ever miss a minute of seeing the twists and turns of life, including enjoying my children. Take in the tree climbing and catching of frogs, the Little League games and the ballet recitals, the driving lessons, the college visits, the first real job.

Unlike the rides at the Mississippi State Fair, you only go on this rollercoaster once.

Keep your eyes open, throw your hands in the air and holler, but don't look back. Enjoy what has come before it passes.

MOVIE REFRESHMENTS

Going to the movies isn't what it used to be.

I remember turning twelve and having to pay $3 for admission instead of $1.50. Back then, popcorn was in the $1 range, and Coca-Colas didn't come in buckets.

Billy Jack and *Shaft* were playing when I was a child, and disaster movies. In the 1970s, there were earthquakes, high-rise buildings burning down, cruise ships flipping over, you name it. I think it went back to the inflation, fuel crisis and angst of the decade . . . life sort of felt disastrous, so seeing an airliner that was hurtling to the ground righted made us all feel better about how much a pound of ground round was going for at Beatty's Big Star.

Not quite all of us, though. My mama was a strict Southern Baptist when it came to movies. She didn't even like that the word "damn" was in *Gone With The Wind*, and would change the channel if "hell" was said on TV. So when it came to movies, getting to go to something PG was a real departure. Maybe to the nether regions, but it was a departure. Disaster movies starring members of the Rat Pack who probably spouted four-letter words were not going to be something we went to see.

G-rated films were usually what I got to see, but she and I did watch a few grown-up movies when I was a small child. I remember *Camelot*, *Funny Girl* and *Dr. Zhivago*. These were a treat not only because some of these were not G-rated, but they finally worked their way to West Point. Getting a first-run movie to town didn't happen until it was on its second or third time around. Maybe fourth. And I loved the rarity of going to the movies with my mother and the comedy of seeing her standards slip for a couple of hours.

Movies got more expensive and permissive as the years went on, and the movie theater in West Point closed, first the Ritz, nicknamed the "Ratz" by us kids, and then another theater that didn't have a proper name like the old movie palaces did.

It became a church for a street preacher who, for a while, would holler at people in the Walmart parking lot nearby, telling them they were going to hell. On a particularly busy day, some might have countered that they had already been there. The preacher had verses across the outside walls of the theater, spelled out letter by letter, screwed into the building's facade. I can't recall the chapters but most likely they were about needing fire insurance for the after life. The letters wouldn't come off easily, or maybe at all, when the church there closed, and it was easier to tear down the theater/church than it was to get the verses off. Being that a building spouting condemnation is a hard sell, down it went.

In later years, my mama and I would still enjoy old movies together, only on the VCR. *It's a*

Wonderful Life was a favorite tape of ours. We's also look at family movies taken decades back, when shooting home movies was high tech, not to mention a pain.

So many of our home movies from back in the day had people standing still in them. It's hard to explain why a camera made to show motion made everyone freeze, but sure enough, there they were with beehive hair and skinny ties, standing, maybe waving if they got a little wild and crazy.

Seeing a movie in a theater is something every child needs as a memory, I don't care how many shows can be streamed from the comfort of home. It's special . . . the trailers, the smell of popcorn, the lights, the Surround-sound.

One Christmas break, we wanted to get out of the house and see a matinee. Money was tight . . . we would have enough to see *Home Alone 3*, but not to get food at the concession counter. And seriously . . . someone could purchase an entire dinner for the cost of movie snacks. Sometimes the snacks are more than the tickets.

Not being able to eat in a movie while watching others walk by with gigantic troughs of popcorn and gallons of Coca-Cola would be close to torture, for me and for my boys.

But it was after Christmas. We had cookies, chocolate, a huge tin of popcorn . . . I decided we would sneak in food, which delighted the boys to no end. The stealthiness of the idea made them giggle. So I got out the largest purse I owned, and we went to work loading it with holiday goodies.

Walking in, I was hoping my bag wasn't giving off the tale-tell scent of baked goods and popped corn, but in we went. Whew . . . we weren't busted.

Then we got into the theater. It was crowded, and we didn't want everyone knowing we were food smugglers, as if the people next to us would point and holler at the sight of our homemade snacks.

A dark movie theater and a loud trailer were the camouflage we needed. The boys, now men, and I still laugh about how we waited until an explosion scene to synchronize the opening of our soda cans.

We then escaped the world for a couple of hours.

COFFEE

Why isn't there coffee-flavored coffee anymore, a friend asked.

Now you can get Irish crème coffee, amaretto coffee, mocha, cinnamon, pumpkin and peppermint.

My second Dear Son's sweet girlfriend works in a coffee shop when she's not finishing a college degree. In that shop, they have blueberry cobbler. Not actual blueberry cobbler, but coffee that tastes like blueberry cobbler. If blueberry cobbler and a cup of coffee married and had a baby, it would be their blueberry cobbler coffee.

There are lattes, half-caffs, dirty chai and espressos. Order a plain cup of coffee, though, my colleague said, and people will look at you like you time-traveled into the future, from, say, the 1950s.

I have a French vanilla medium roast, that, with enough skim milk and Splenda, is addictive. I make sure that the coffee maker is loaded before I go to sleep, so all I have to do is hit the switch in the morning. Which, before my caffeine, is asking a lot.

Love of coffee is new to me. My parents drank it by the pot every morning. Some of the first sounds in the house were the perks from the percolator.

Coffee, I learned, smelled wonderful. It tasted like the most bitter, awful sludge in the world, though, when I was a child. My daddy let me try it. He grew up on a farm, and all the kids had chores to do before they walked to school, so I suspect that he and my uncles were drinking coffee as soon as they could walk.

All during my growing-up years, coffee was a joke between us. He'd laugh every time I would try to drink it, only to make a face. Why, you ask, would I keep trying it, if it was horrible? Because everyone else in the world drinks coffee.

Now you know. I am a lemming when it comes to coffee.

After a while, I settled with drinking hot tea or cocoa, or that breakfast drink of champions, Diet Coke, but in my adulthood, I kept getting faced with free coffee. Seldom do you see free tea or free soft drinks, but free coffee is everywhere. You could be flat broke and still have a coffee habit.

My inner tightwad was intrigued.

I would take Pearl the Civic to the car dealer for service because of, what else, free coffee and cookies. Doesn't everyone pick their mechanics that way? If you offer me wi-fi plus white chocolate

143

macadamia nut cookies and coffee with fancy creamer, my car and I will be on your doorstep every 3,000 miles.

And then there are company meetings. They sometimes have free coffee. You don't want to look like some non-coffee-drinking pansy at a meeting. I didn't, so I drank the coffee. For free.

Hotels and supermarkets have free coffee, too. I tried some at The Fresh Market that was a peach-flavored summer blend. Upscale places usually don't have coffee-flavored coffee. Their coffee has to taste like something plus coffee with Turbinado sugar on the side.

Somewhere along the line, I began liking coffee so much I would pay for it. Now, sitting on my deck first thing in the morning with a large cup of coffee is a moment of sanity in my day. I like to wake up with grateful thoughts, and right after being grateful for my children and my gentleman friend, I think thoughts about how good that coffee tastes.

Sanity, it turns out, does not taste like the toxic sludge it used to. I acquired the taste for bitter brown liquid with grit in it. I now consider it something nice I do for myself.

The older Dear Sons acquired the taste in college. As a student at Southern Miss, the oldest Dear Son had $700 in available credit at the combination student bookstore and Starbucks. I think most of the charges were at Starbucks.

His brother has a fancy-shmancy Keurig coffee maker. He's called it life changing and even travels with it. He loves his girlfriend and his guitar. I am thinking that third on his love list might be the Keurig.

I use that coffee maker of my daddy's, the one I kept on the kitchen counter for years after he died. It's back in the spot where he used it, and I enjoy thinking about him every time I pour a cup.

He'd probably laught about me liking the taste of coffee now, because he loved me, laughing and coffee.

The coffee-flavored kind.

SOAP OPERAS

Back when I was growing up, my mama had a basket of clothes that she'd take out when her stories were on. She'd set the ironing board up, get a glass Coca-Cola bottle filled with water and topped with a shaker lid and her iron. This was before there were steam irons and wrinkle-free fabrics.

She'd get to work smoothing out the wrinkles on my daddy's shirts while the stories unfolded. These were soap operas, or what the Emmys like to call "daytime dramas."

I grew up watching them, first on a little black-and-white TV in the kitchen, then later on a color set. I didn't really start paying much attention to them until my mama hired a teenager or two to keep me from playing with matches and running with scissors while she ran errands.

These girls were in high school and wore flared jeans. They plucked their eyebrows and ironed their hair instead of someone's shirts. I thought they were the coolest people to walk the earth, and they watched "The Young and The Restless.' ' This was back when David Hasselhoff was a character named Trapper on there, and he had not yet taken up running in slow motion on the beach or being creepy.

The cool older kids liked this daytime drama, which had lots of people in it who wore flared jeans and platform shoes. My mama was more of an "As The World Turns'' woman, and I don't recall too many people even having a pair of jeans in that show. There was always someone half dead and hanging on by a thread while almost everyone else looked on in horror. Those not looking on in horror had wicked smiles as they were planning to celebrate the poor patient's demise.

Of course, I became a "Y&R''fan instead, keeping up with the Mrs. Chancellor vs. Jill drama, which pretty much spanned all the summers of my childhood. Mrs. Chancellor was a wealthy alcoholic whose husband took up with Jill, who was hired to be a companion to Mrs. C and most likely to keep her and Jim Beam apart. She failed miserably, giving Mrs. Chancellor another reason to drink as she took up with her husband.

See how addicting these shows can be? This was a plot to the show from decades ago, and I still remember it.

Later, in my teens, my best friends were "General Hospital'' fans. This was during the "Luke and Laura" craze and when Rick Springfield was playing Dr. Noah Drake while simultaneously having a hit album on the pop charts. So needless to say, we were hooked. We'd wean ourselves off "General Hospital'' when school started in the late summer, and then catch up during holidays and spring break.

But during the summer, we'd watch every day. We'd make a snack, pour a glass of Coca-Cola and stare intently at the TV screen, anxious to find out if Celia Quartermane had married the real Dr. Grant Putnam or his evil twin who was really a spy.

We'd call each other on the phone so we could talk to each other about the show while we were watching the show. Because it was important for us to tell each other we thought John Stamos' character "Blackie'' was cute. It was imperative for us to talk each other through momentous occasions such as weddings and holiday parties, which always meant something was about to go down.

No one on a soap opera can have any event past a Bastille Day picnic without a major throw-down, knock-down or drag-out. It is spelled out in the writers' contracts.

At my days at Mississippi University for Women, there would be "Spuds and Suds'' parties where one of the student groups would make baked potatoes for lunch, and the participants would catch up on their soaps between classes.

And then I graduated, married and became a mama myself. I did love me some soaps back when I was a freelance writer and stay-at-home mom. I was too Young and Restless to be Bold and

Beautiful, and I was watching "All My Children" while watching all my children.

My own mama was industrious, ironing her way through the stories. It was her way of saying, "You know, I wouldn't be watching this except that I am ironing my husband's work shirts like the good wife that I am."

No ironing for me. I was parked with my hiner in the recliner, a sandwich in hand, when my stories came on. Whatever writing or housework had to be done was going to wait an hour, and unless one of the kids was bleeding or setting fire to something, they were going to take a number.

This was my sanity back then. Soap opera people lived in a world of adult conversations, where people shook up cocktails instead of chocolate milk. All you mamas with young children, you will totally get this. It was a glimpse into another world that didn't have any big purple dinosaurs in it.

Now I did also take in my share of 1980s evening soaps. "Falcon Crest" and "Dallas" and "Dynasty," and yes, back in the day, my friends and I would have to call to get each other's take on whatever Crystal or Alexis had done to each other. Usually it involved a claws-out cat fight in the middle of a cocktail party or society reception.

You couldn't take those two anywhere without them turning a garden party into a barroom brawl. What'd I say about that writers' contract?

Alas, I have given up soaps. The Boss Man at the office tends to frown on me having a TV set going while pretending to work.

But I did get hooked on some "Downton Abbey," and "House of Cards." Now newcomers such as Hulu Plus and Netflix have started trotting out cliffhangers where they put all thirteen episodes of a season on at the same time, ensuring that most people will have a 13-hour TV-watching marathon.

As for PBS and "Downton Abbey,'' a classy soap but a soap nonetheless, they have solved their funding problems. I didn't watch Season 3 because I was catching up with Season 2 and didn't want any spoilers. Now I have to buy Season 3 and download it to find out what happens to Anna and Mr. Bates.

And you know I will.

Part 4

Home Sweet Home

BATHROOMS

My bathroom just has the basics.

A tub, a commode, a sink and a door.

Yet, when my children were small, it might as well have been a spa to me if I could be in there by myself.

Some women value diamonds. Others wish for flashy cars, a new wardrobe or a trip to Europe. Mamas of young children are happy with just uninterrupted bathroom time and occasionally sleeping past 7 a.m. Taking a shower without having to deal with a screaming child is more magical than a unicorn dipped in glitter.

My children could be totally fine. Sleeping, drawing pictures, maybe watching a big purple dinosaur on TV. Happy and peaceful.

Then I would get the bright idea to wash my hair. Putting shampoo on my head was like throwing a match to gasoline when it came to my children. In their younger days, all I had to do was start sudsing, and they would immediately start trying to kill each other. The two oldest Dear Sons, who I should have named Cain and Abel, would start hollering at each other.

"Moooooommmmm!" one would scream.

I would pray no one was bleeding and go tromping out of my refuge dressed in towels, or, if they didn't sound desperate enough, I might counter with the threat of "Don't you make me come out there."

There would be little fingers reaching under the bathroom door. If I forgot to lock the door, they might, in a moment of lunacy caused by me spending 10 minutes on myself, walk in on me with their wailing, which would then result in me hollering, but that rarely ever happened.

Why? Because I knew that a lock on the bathroom door was the only thing between me and losing it some days. I might misplace car keys. I might forget to buy cat food or lose my glasses or my cell phone. But I rarely ever would forget to lock the bathroom door.

I realized I had become a mama the day I took a shower and only shaved one leg. I didn't realize it for the better part of a day.

Now I have a teen and a tween. One would think two bathrooms for three people would be plenty, but one would be mistaken.

There's at least a fight a week over bathroom space. No one wants to climb the stairs to the second bathroom, so if I am in the downstairs bath and the kids need it, the barging in, banging on the door or hollering commences. Depending on how close it is to the time the school bus rounds the corner, I might get all three from the Dear Son and the Dear Daughter.

Hair, for them, is an important thing. That, and scent. You can always tell when a teenage boy has been in a bathroom. There are wet towels on the floor and a cloud of Axe body spray hanging in the air like a fog. It's amazing girls at the high school can breathe.

Now the door-locking happens between brother and sister, too. After years of twisting, our doorknob gave up. One evening, the Dear Daughter, having locked out the world or at least her older brother, went to unlock it, but nothing. The doorknob would just spin.

Mama and her gentleman friend had gone to the movies that night, so she was left to holler for help to her teenage brother, who was so busy playing video games that he didn't hear her. That's his story, and he's sticking to it.

So then, being the resourceful girl that she is, the Dear Daughter unlocked the bathroom window, pulled herself up and jumped down to the deck in the back yard.

She later decided to brush her hair, which could qualify as an upper-body workout. Her brother, passing by in the hall and claiming to have been oblivious to her daring escape from the locked bathroom, closed the door on her and, according to the Dear Daughter, ran and laughed.

Their accounts differ on this as well.

To keep everyone from locking everyone out of the downstairs bath, I took the doorknob off. We were then left with a bathroom door with a hole where the doorknob should go. The Dear Daughter stuffs washcloths into it as if the rest of us are Peeping Toms.

She says we have no shame since we take the chance that our family members are not voyeurs and don't block the view from the hole in the door.

Of course, we could just walk upstairs to the second bathroom, but that would require walking upstairs. Such a crazy thought. I could use that bathroom as my own spa get-away, but then I would have to also walk upstairs.

Installing a new doorknob to the downstairs bath is at the top of the family to-do list, mainly for its peace-keeping properties. There's one requirement—it's got to lock and unlock.

GARDENS

Growing a vegetable garden is a trendy thing to do these days.

Michelle Obama has one at the White House. Michael Pollan writes books about eating close to home, and you can't get much closer to home than your own back yard. All the hip little magazines about cottages for people who don't live in them have vegetable gardens in them, either planning them, planting them or picking not just normal produce out of them, but heirloom vegetables.

Heirloom vegetables means that they either look a little off, say the tomatoes come out purple instead of red, or that they have a neat story that comes with them about how they were cultivated. I bought one that was called "Mortgage Lifter" because it was developed in the 1930s by a man who used the proceeds to pay off his mortgage. I'd have just been happy with a few tomatoes, as "Mortgage Lifter" didn't like my yard.

Years ago, people stopped going into their back yards for their veggies and instead went to the supermarket, and this meant that veggies had to stay pretty longer. When veggies needed to stay fresh a long time off the vine or out of the ground, then the kinds of veggies that didn't hang on that long were tossed by the wayside, along with the unusual and the just plain weird. Time was, having tasteless but fresh and nearly identical veggies was the thing.

Now it is hip to have the just plain weird again. I mean, who wants a red tomato when you can have yellow or orange?

At our place, we plant a tiny garden every year. It is tiny in a ratio to the width of my lazy streak. I do this because I, too, want to be hip enough to have dirt under my fingernails, yet I try to keep things on a small enough scale to keep it fun. I can weed a small garden patch and have fun.

Kids also enjoy gardening. They love the idea of planting seeds. They don't love the idea of weeding or hoeing, and some parts of going organic they were befuddled about.

Once, we were working in some organic matter into the ground. It was manure. It was in a pile, and we were taking hoes to work it into the dirt.

"I smell poop,'' one of the Dear Sons said.

"Well, yeah,'' I said. "That's what manure is. Poop.''

They stood open-mouthed at the thought I would have the family poking at poop so we could then plant seeds in it.

"Ewww.''

One Dear Son said, "I can't believe you went to the store and bought poop in a bag."

155

Whether your kids learn what manure is or not, they will actually eat the vegetables that come out of your yard. Sometimes.

I did have one Dear Son, by this time a college student, who hated the idea of eating what he called "yard salad."

"You don't know what's been in that garden," he said, insinuating it might be a litter box for every stray cat in the neighborhood.

"I wash everything," I said. "And you don't know what's been in the factory farm."

That last line had me feeling like I should just go buy a Prius, stop shaving my armpits and move to San Francisco.

"And tomatoes grow higher than cats can tee-tee," I added.

He couldn't argue with logic like that. Nobody could. That might be the reason they call it organic gardening.

I can't help but think of my forefathers when I try to garden in our itty-bitty-trendy organic garden. I'm only a generation removed from the farm. Back when my daddy, we'll call him Grandpa here, was growing up, if they didn't grow it, they didn't eat it.

I am ready to say right here and now that if our family had to grow whatever we lived on, we'd all be goners.

Grandpa had the luxury of being a little picky as an adult, but let me tell you, if it came out of the ground when he was growing up, it got eaten. The garden we have might get us some heirloom tomatoes and a few cucumbers and summer squash, but the family farming skills skipped over me. If we had to depend on what came out of our own little patch of suburban land, we might get one little yard salad before we all passed out from hunger.

Now it's sort of a treat, these home-grown goodies. The Gentleman Friend had me over for spaghetti made with fresh herbs from the garden at his place, and another time, he cooked fresh green beans with garlic.

It's not so much sustenance, as we get that from the supermarket. It's something special. Back in my grandparents' day, we'd have had to flip that. Treats were store-bought, and sustenance came out of the ground.

Getting a little dirt under the fingernails may not do wonders for your manicure, but since I don't have one, I don't care. And while it is trendy, we've liked playing in the dirt before it became hip.

For us, it's a way to connect to where we came from and have a little appreciation for our past, when arguments at my daddy's home would be about how many rows of turnip greens were going to be planted. My grandfather favored planting a field of one thing, while my grandmother wanted a row of this and a row of that. Because God does have a sense of humor, the folks who say "I dos" to each other will be a mix of field people and row people.

Field or row, I am thinking my grandparents would have been quite entertained at the thought of gardening being hip. If they would have understood that "hip" was something other than the intersection of "leg" and "belly."

They knew, and I know, that when you stick a fork into something you grew out of your own piece of ground, the blessing that came before it is just a little more meaningful. We know where what we said grace over came from.

HOMETOWNS

A lot of who you are comes from where you're from. It's your base of reference. Everything that comes after is compared to what came before. Who you think you are, what's in your heart, how you think and feel, when you get up and when you turn in and everything that happens in between, how you raise your children and what you dream of all comes from where you came from.

And that is home.

There's a lot of truth to the saying that it takes a village to raise a child. In my case, it took a small town to raise me.

When I was growing up, if you started doing some shenanigans—and all of us did—the grownups in town took it upon themselves to get onto you. And tell your mama. That meant that you would get in trouble again once you got home, because having another adult complain about you to your mama was like a curse to the whole family. Or so it was portrayed. That keeps you honest and responsible. Or else.

I grew up in the town my father grew up in, and in the same house, too.

So that meant I got to hear stories about him and my uncles. I remember a lady at the local drug store telling me how she taught my daddy how addition and subtraction worked by counting out penny candy.

Since my daddy had a knack for adding sums up in his head without a pencil or paper to help, I figured he was born knowing how. Imagining him as a little boy was hard, but somehow funny to me back then. Kids always think of their parents as being put on this earth as 40-year-olds, like children were the ones who invented being children.

Home is a comforting word, or should be. It is where you can kick your shoes off and be yourself. It's where people not only ask about your mama, but they wait to hear your answer. Home is where, when there's been a sickness or death in someone's family, everyone else's ovens heat up to 350 degrees awaiting the casseroles that will be coming to your house.

That's your home and your hometown. It is where you don't need to read the street signs because you know where you're going and could get there blindfolded.

It's where, when you feel like you don't know what you're doing, everyone else does. In a time where we had three TV channels at the most, the real entertainment was keeping up with what everyone was doing.

The prayer list in the church bulletin had the names of the sick people in town, and the local newspaper used to publish the names of the really sick people who made it to the local hospital. There

159

were also stories back then about who had family in town for a visit, who had a bridal shower, and who showed up with a toaster.

That may sound like a massive invasion of privacy, but to us, it wasn't. Call it being nosy or call it caring about those we shared our hometown with. There are worse things than growing up knowing people around you, even the ones who told your mama you were running in the grocery store cared about you.

It also makes you authentic to grow up in a hometown, or if you're from the city, substitute in the word "neighborhood," where everyone knows your business. It keeps you real. It's pointless to try to be anything other than what you are in your hometown because everyone knows the truth anyway—and loves you in spite of it.

Your hometown is where your neighbors, friends and family claim you as one of their own. It's where you belong.

Hometowns can make you dream big dreams. For one thing, dreaming big dreams was something for us to do in those pre-cable days. It was great fun. We'd dream of leaving our little hometown, and some of us did. Others stuck around and chased their dreams closer to home. But no dreaming, near or far, would have been done without us having some deep roots. You can chase dreams better when you know you have a hometown that will either be there to cheer you on or will dust you off if you crash land.

Hometowns are where each of us learned to play, where we learned how to love, hurt, forgive and go on. It taught us who we were so we can become who we're going to be. It gave us the gifts we needed to grow, and it's those that we're passing along to our own children, who most likely think we never lived a day in our lives as a child.

Having left my hometown eighteen years ago, it's a little sad when I come back. The home where my older sons spent part of their childhood is where other people's children are playing. The house where I grew up, and where my mama and daddy lived in their retirement are homes to other people, now. Most likely, I don't know them.

I can drive around and ooh and ahh about what's changed and what stayed the same since the last time I was around. When you're in your hometown, change is ice-meltingly slow, but when you haven't been there for a while, the change is all you see.

There's a tattoo parlor downtown now, and a flower shop over there that used to be the Sears & Roebuck.

And you think about the past, and the good times, and how your boy used to roll down the steep hill and climb the wisteria in the park like you did. You remember festivals and street dances and regular old days that didn't stand out at the time.

You realize how going back home, really going back, is something you can only do in your memories.

CELL PHONES

I didn't want to be a belled cat.

When I was at work, I wanted to work, and when I was home, I wanted to be home. I had what most newspaper reporters and editors develop over time, an intense distaste for being found when not working. When that happens, it is never the Prize Patrol van on the lookout for you. It only means something awful has happened and something equally awful is about to happen to your off hours.

It's not impossible, but it's much harder to find a cat un-belled with no jingle-jangle to tip someone off. But technology has jingle-jangled us all. First I had to wear a pager. I admit, it was cool to wear it, like I was a brain surgeon on call, but I was happy when it didn't go off.

Then there were cellphones. I saw some moms with them, and they never stopped talking on them. Ever. They talked in the car, on the way into church, on the way into work, throughout ballet recitals and baseball games.

I really didn't want to be one of them. I had to talk on the phone at work, but I didn't see any reason why I'd want to carry a phone with me so I could talk on the phone even more. I didn't even want to talk on the phone when I was paid to do so.

That was until I had a cat of my own that needed to be belled. A teenage son driving made me want a cellphone in the worst way. Until he discovered texting and overages.

I think he texted the world and God, because our bill was $400 one month. This was one of many instances that has proven my love for the oldest Dear Son, because he is alive today. If I wasn't a woman of faith, I might have killed him.

These were primative phones. Archaeologists already see these and proclaim them relics of an earlier civilization. You know, the early 2000s.

They were stupid phones, not smartphones. All they did was make phone calls and send text messages. We were practically Neanderthals then, what with our clothing styles left over from the 1990s and few if any apps.

I still have a stupid phone. They may not do much other than call and provide a portable alarm clock, but they are practically indestructible. Mine has fallen a zillion times only to be put back together again in perfect working order.

In contrast, I got an iPhone assigned to me from work. It was not so much for talking on the phone or texting, but for shooting video and taking photographs. I was crazy enough to take it running with me once, and laid it on a post by the running trail. Somehow it nosedived off and has been cracked ever since. It is bone china, when I live in a bull rampage world. Amazingly, it still shoots good videos and photos, and its phone calls aren't bad, either.

Socially, it is a settler of questions. If the gentleman friend and I are discussing movies, and I can't think of an actor's name, there he is, whipping out his iPhone and checking the internet.

Now the whole family has cell phones on a family plan. A couple hundred bucks a month for the kids and I to keep in touch, and it goes like this.

The oldest Dear Son tries not to use his at work, which is admirable. The middle Dear Son and I are never on the same schedule, so when he calls, I miss it, and I forget and call him during class. The youngest Dear Son has been known to jump into swimming pools with his phones, or leave them in pants pockets for me to wash, but I get him replacements that he forgets to charge or leaves at home. The Dear Daughter just loses her phone. Once enough time has passed for it to go dead, we just hope she stumbles upon it, because calling her number to locate the phone will do no good.

They wonder why I won't get them iPhones, which, if it were not for my job, I wouldn't have.

Smartphones are more expensive to replace.

Plus, the youngest members of our family plan lose, destroy or forget their phones, making me wonder why I am laying out the long green for the family plan when I am the only one of us in our house who carries the phone around on a regular basis.

I pay a high price for being belled.

MOWING YARDS

The other day at the office, I got this email about a new invention. An air-conditioned lawnmower.

I was thinking the only thing better than this might be a riding vacuum cleaner that dispenses dark chocolate, chardonnay and $100 bills. But yes, right here in Ridgeland, there is an air-conditioned lawnmower.

I am thinking the inventor may have found his million-dollar idea because lawn mowing is not easy. Or fun. And the air is not conditioned. It's like a whiff of hell during most of the summer.

I tend to do most of our mowing, though, because I like the feeling of accomplishment, as lap by lap of the yard, more grass is cut down to size. I may be sweaty when it's done, but the grass is short and the neighbors won't think the single mom's house is the worst one on the block.

I once was introduced to a neighbor from down the street. He immediately said, "You're that girl I've seen mowing the yard.'' And then talked about me being a sweaty mess.

It's always nice to leave an impression. Mine is one of sweat and short grass.

I do hit a point, though, where my definition of "done'' goes from perfection to not passing out in the front yard. The weeds are no longer weeds. I declare them "a meadow.''

The Clarion-Ledger garden columnist and radio personality Felder Rushing once wrote that it is being kind to the bees to leave white clover growing in your yard.

I hit a point in my lawn care where I no longer care whether the clover's short. In fact, I want the little white flowers showing. I reach a point when I want to be kind to the bees. And drink something cold while the air conditioner blows on me.

There are some endearing things about Southern men. One is that they don't like to have people see their women mowing the yard. I don't think it's so much that they mind us doing the mowing. It's just that the sight of women in the family mowing the grass makes them look bad.

One of the oldest Dear Son's friends threatened him with a knock-down drag-out if he saw me mowing the yard. Just because, in his teenage Southern male mind, my oldest boy was making the whole family look bad by mama being seen with her dainty hands on a push mower.

The youngest Dear Son, if he hears me cut the mower on, will come out to mow, but I think it is because he's hoping there's money involved later. His ulterior motives don't matter to me. I call it chivalrous and let go of the mower handle.

My sweet gentleman friend, while I was out of town visiting my oldest, grown-uppest Dear Sons, mowed my yard and fixed a leaky pipe. Ladies, that is a display of love. Any idiot can go buy roses, but a man mowing your yard as a surprise is putting sweat equity into the relationship. Lots of sweat equity in the gentleman friend's case as he did this in late July.

Once we lived across the street from a family where the mama did do the mowing, and she would work on her tan by jumping on their riding lawn mower in a bikini. None of the men in the neighborhood seemed to mind her mowing. In fact, in a similar fashion to Pavlov's dogs, the mere sound of her mower cranking up would send them outside to do chores. They would do those chores shirtless, simultaneously sucking in their guts and flexing their biceps.

Then there was a fellow Mississippi University for Women student I knew who would mow the yard at her family's home. She was a member of the modeling squad on campus, and it showed. She would have full makeup, cute white shorts with matching super-white Keds, all the rage back then, and a matching pair of socks, T-shirt and hair bow. It was disgusting how cute she was.

I think she willed herself not to perspire. Besides, at the school we called The W, women didn't sweat. Mississippi University for Women students only glisten. I'd have been glistening so much the makeup would have slid right off my face.

When I mow, I don't wear a bikini. If I did, my mama would rise up from the dead to personally wear me out. I don't dress cute and wear makeup, either.

I sweat like a field hand. Or since I am an MUW graduate, I glisten like a field hand.

The Dear Daughter has taken a try at mowing, but she stops just as the first bead of sweat, aka glistening dew, forms on her little forehead.

Even though the youngest Dear Son is still home with me, I get out and mow with the push mower. It's like getting a workout while getting the grass shorter, and I am all about multitasking.

I wear old T-shirts and jeans with holes in them and the oldest, nastiest running shoes in the house. Because cute clothes are for seeing friends, but these clothes . . . they are for doing battle. They are for kicking the butts of thousands upon thousands of blades of grass.

If the Dear Son doesn't come to stop me, I keep making laps up and down the yard until I give out or run out of tall grass. Then, when I drive past our house, I either take a little pride in the front yard's appearance or note that I have a little too much "meadow" along the sides.

ZUCCHINI

I grew up giving thanks over food, but few things will make you as thankful for those forkfuls like gardening.

My grandfather was a farmer, and even though he had passed on before I was even thought about, I think about him when I plant what I call the itty-bitty garden each spring.

Careful not to plant before Good Friday or risk being hit by what my daddy used to call the Easter Spell, the last blast of winter, I put out little tomato plants and mound up dirt into hills for squash and cucumber seeds. I get a few dinner sides out of playing in the dirt, but my grandfather planted just about everything his large family put in their mouths. We'd starve if our family had to depend on my gardening skills.

Except for that one year I planted zucchini.

"Oh, yeah," said a friend of mine in West Point that year. "If you want to feel like a master gardener, plant zucchini."

She told me that after I planted a whole row of zucchini. I had such a talent for killing tomato plants that I figured I needed to plant some spares to get a few good squash for the grill.

No, that year, they grew like kudzu. Never before or since have nature and dirt conspired to create the perfect conditions for zucchini in our yard. They started out as orange-yellow flowers with greenish hips, then the next day, there would be a zucchini, as if the zucchini fairy waved a wand over my back yard overnight. Miss picking a zucchini and it was growing to monstrous proportions in a couple more days.

Now there are a few things I dislike doing. Throwing away food is one of them, especially food I got dirty and sweaty for. Garden food should be eaten if at all possible.

We know that overgrown okra is a no, as it will prove to be inedible. Take a bite of old okra, and you will come as close to knowing what chewing a cud is like without actually being a cow. It can't be swallowed.

Broccoli gone to flower can be eaten. I did it, convincing myself I was eating some hipster vegetable. You watch . . . some celebrity chef will have some broccoli go to flower and then all of a sudden, flowered broccoli will be the in thing and farmers will let it sit in the ground a while longer before picking.

Call me anything but a zucchini waster.

When the zucchini first came in, it was heralded with much excitement. We had sauteed zucchini, grilled zucchini, shish-ka-bobbed zucchini, squash casserole. Then the new began to wear off.

I cooked the zucchini, then scooped out the inside, mixed it with onion and tomato, topped it with parmesan cheese and declared it twice-baked zucchini. I baked zucchini bread and a chocolate cake that had zucchini as its secret ingredient. I made bread and butter pickles out of zucchini.

Zucchini was fast becoming something to sneak into dinner instead of one of the stars of the plate. The kids would nearly run from the table if they saw anything that might resemble a squash. Even I was finding zucchini a little hard to stomach.

But then there is the tradition of sharing homegrown produce. Even better than having a garden is having a friend with one, because then you get some veggies without having to till, plant, weed or pick. When you have an embarrassment of riches in your garden, you share.

That year, I wasn't giving away tomatoes or green beans. I was giving away zucchini. Anyone who left their car windows down in town might return to find a few squash riding shotgun. I gave them to policemen and firefighters. I gave then away to neighbors. I stopped short at leaving them in a basket on someone's doorstep, ringing the bell and running.

But summers come and summers go. Before long, the zucchini plants withered away, and squash became fewer and fewer.

And like we did for the presence of homegrown tomatoes and pink-eye-purple hulls, we gave thanks for the squash's departure.

NEVER RUN AWAY FROM HOME

Years ago, there was a little boy who was angry with his mama.

Really angry.

Who'd she think she was, anyway, telling him to take naps and not play in the street? He had enough of that heifer, and at the ripe old age of three, he decided he was going to run away. Then she would be sorry.

A clean shirt, some Legos and a truck or two. It was all going into a tote bag, his version of the bandana on a stick.

He was busy packing when I discovered the plot.

"I'm running away," the oldest Dear Son declared, "and you can't stop me."

"I'm not going to stop you," I said. "I just need to pack a few things to take along. Where are we going?"

"You can't come, mama," he said. "It doesn't work that way."

"Sure it does," I said. "I'll just pack us a snack for later, and we'll leave a note for your daddy."

"Well, if you're going to come, then I might as well stay home."

And a little boy's attempt at running away from home was thwarted.

After all, if your mama's going to ruin your good time, she might as well just ruin your good time without you having to leave home. It's more convenient that way.

I know, because my mama ruined plenty of fun for me, too. She'd tell me no and make me go to church and go to bed, and when I wanted to run away, I didn't get to do that, either.

Running away from home is pointless. Whether mama's going to pack up and go with you or do like mine did and turn you around at the door and send you back into your room to unpack, attempts at runing away are futile.

For starters, if you're running away, you're way too young to handle what's out there in the big world. How do you know that what you're running to isn't worse than what you're running from? For three-year-old boys, an attempt at running away nearly always results in a new-found appreciation for mama and her rules and dinner. Let's not forget dinner. Even baths are bearable after contemplating life on the lam.

For grown people, facing problems is better than running from them. Hiding from troubles, avoiding them, pretending they don't exist are all forms of running away. Amazing that adults have figured out how to run away from home without ever leaving. That way you can keep change to a minimum.

The problem with this is that you keep change to a minimum, including change for the better. Ignored troubles only get bigger and hairier.

The other problem is that your troubles may be something you're carrying around in your very own personal bandana on a stick. You can try to run from some things, but you can't run away from yourself. If the big, hairy problem is not so much where you are or the situation you're in but your own outlook or choices or decisions, then the farther you run, the more your big, hairy problem will be gaining on you.

The process of trying to run away from your own self is just exhausting, and not in a good way, like running on a tree-lined trail exhausting. It's more like running on a hamster wheel treadmill exhausting, having nothing to show for your sweat. No matter where you run to, there you are.

The other thing about running away from home is that home tends to stay with you. Just like your own self and your own thoughts and choices. Home is a part of you.

It's been a long time since I lived in the home I grew up in, and my parents have been in glory for years and years, but in the things I do, from coffee in the morning to doing laundry on certain days to enjoying time outside, I see the life my parents lived and my home. If I moved a dozen times, the thoughts I think, the memories, the mannerisms, would all go with me, even if I tried my hardest to leave them behind.

Running away from home never works.

The best option is just what the little boy did. He let someone who loves him unpack his baggage, he talked about his troubles until they were all gone, and then he ate a bowl of chocolate ice cream.

Years ago, there was a woman who went missing in a neighboring city. When she didn't show up at work, the authorities came to her house and immediately suspected foul play. They took one look around and thought that the home had been ransacked and that a hellacious battle had ensued.

As the investigation continued, news reports contradicted the lawmen's first hypothesis. There wasn't a knock-down drag-out in her home. It turns out she just wasn't a very good housekeeper.

This is a cautionary tale, people. Don't let this happen to you.

Forget wearing clean underwear in case you're in an accident. You need to have your house or apartment in some sort of order before you leave for the day just so if you're kidnapped, the law officers won't swear to tell the truth, the whole truth and nothing but the truth and then testify at your kidnapper's trial that your house was a mess.

I have never had OCD when it came to housework. I have been known to watch "Hoarders" just to make myself feel like a better housekeeper.

My attitude has been that my children aren't going to want my attention forever, so I should enjoy them now, much to the disdain of my late husband, who shall be known as Baby Daddy.

One night, Baby Daddy said something about the house being a trainwreck while I was rocking the oldest, an arm baby at the time.

"The mess will still be there, but the baby won't," I said.

"Yeah, I believe the mess will still be there. It'll be there tomorrow and the next day, too."

Another cautionary tale: Men, please don't say things like this. It leads to loneliness and sleeping on the couch.

Another time, when I was a newspaper reporter with two small children, there was quite a bit of news going on and Baby Daddy had a bad knee. My mama, known in this story as Grandma, came over to watch the two sweet grandboys so Baby Daddy could stay off his feet and I could cover a public hearing on a landfill. Be sure to catch the irony of what I was assigned to cover.

I was fully aware of the state of our home, so I was ready to hear testimony on garbage. It was a bad week. The dishes were stacked high enough in the sink to be seen through the kitchen window. It looked like the kids' toy box exploded, throwing Legos to all four corners. The house was a full-scale disaster.

"You just enjoy those boys," I told Grandma. "Don't touch the housework."

And she did enjoy those boys. And she didn't touch the housework.

What happened next wasn't quite as bad as being kidnapped with a messy house, but it was close.

The preacher came over.

Now, I am quite fond of this particular preacher, and really just about all ministers. But preachers have awful timing. They never come over when your house is together, the children are clean and there's a baking sheet of tea cakes coming out of your oven. No, the preacher comes over, appropriately, I suppose, when all hell is breaking loose.

Our preacher came over that evening to check on Baby Daddy and his bad knee. And then, I am guessing, offered up prayers for us all.

"Annie," the preacher said on the phone the next day, "is everything alright?"

"Sure," I said. "We're just fine."

Because this is what Southerners say even if their heads are half attached.

He then asked if I needed some of the women of the church to come over to help with the house since I was working and Baby Daddy was limping around.

It was a kind offer, but I was mortified. Not quite as much as if he'd have been under oath and in open court, but still.

I've gotten better at keeping the house under control, which has coincided with the children growing up, so draw your own conclusions there. Having a clean house is just about impossible when your children are small. I just did the best I could.

Hiring someone to clean would have been pointless unless it was someone like Alice from "The Brady Bunch" who lived at our house and worked 24/7, because small children are pretty much wrecking crews. A clean house with them in it stays clean fifteen minutes, tops.

But what really matters? Things or people? I have a philosophy that I got from the mom of my oldest son's best friend in elementary school, a wise woman with a not-so-perfect house.

"I worry about how people feel in my home and not so much what they see," she said one day when her place wasn't exactly ready for the photographer from Southern Living.

For me, that was a housekeeping epiphany.

Ever since that conversation, I have not shyed away from opening the door. If you want to see us, come on over. If you want to see the house, make an appointment a week in advance.

After my sons got old enough to date, one was telling me about a girlfriend's home. It sounded beautiful, the showroom-like furniture, the kitchen right out of a scene from a magazine spread, the lack of clutter. But then family members were yelling at each other over a small mess that, seriously, would not have even registered on the Richter scale at the Oeth home.

"I wanted to hide under the carpet," he said.

Our place is miles from perfect but we try not to yell unless the house is on fire. Nobody hides under the carpet, and if they did, who knows what they might find under there.

Like I told Baby Daddy about children, they aren't around forever. When your babies are grown, I promise you they won't remember how clean your house was. They won't remember if the furniture was flawless, the dishes were done and the floor was swept.

What will stick in their memories was whether your home was fun, how at ease they felt and how no one minded if they had a bunch of friends over, and you do want them to have their friends over.

How I want people to feel in our home is at home. At ease. And I try to keep it clean enough to be comfortable and fun, but not enough to turn me into a shrew. Together enough so there are clean dishes for when we decide to make tacos and have company over at the last minute and fresh jeans and T-shirts for school each morning, but not so perfect that no one can kick off their shoes and watch a movie. Clean enough to be comfy for the people who call this place home, yet messy enough to be a place to make fun memories.

POP-A-MATIC TROUBLE

It may start as an innocent family game night. Just a little Pop-a-Matic Trouble. It's this simple little game board with plastic thimble-like pieces that get moved around until they arrive at home. The dice is even in a protective Pop-a-Matic bubble.

It's deceptive in its appeal. It seems like the sort of game little children can play with ease, and they can. A child who can count to six can participate, but vengefulness comes out to play because the thimbles, if landed on by another, can be sent back to start over from scratch, even if they are just the roll of a one away from being safe at home.

Trouble is addictive. Adults in our family play, and Katie, bar the door on Christmas Eve. Playing a family Pop-a-Matic tournament has become a tradition that might land my children in counseling one day.

"Doctor, it was awful. We'd play Trouble after the Christmas Eve service, and my brother would always send me back. On purpose."

"Mom could have avoided jumping me, but I'm not the favorite."

"I hate my family."

I can imagine it all now.

As a friend of the family once said, "It's not a Pop-a-Matic Trouble game until someone cries." It's as close to a live Jerry Springer show as my house ever gets.

Another issue with Trouble is that you will not move off your home row to start the game until you roll a six. Sixes are not easy to roll, but then they come in bunches. At our house, we call you the Anti-Christ if you roll three sixes in a roll. Usually the roller of 666 does an evil laugh.

But you might also sit, roll a two, watch everyone else race their thimbles around the board, sit, roll a four, and watch the cycle continue, wondering if you're ever going to see a six. And when you do get one, a happy dance ensues.

Getting onto the board means you roll moves until you are home free and have smited your nearest and dearest into the land of Trouble loserdom.

Just watching the siblings play is a chilling thing. If looks could kill, our whole family would have been goners a long time ago, thanks to that aptly named game.

We also get pretty lively when we play Uno, which usually ends with me questioning how someone could make the woman who gave him life draw four, but Uno has not engendered the passion among us that Trouble has.

People who don't play don't get it.

Once, during a family Trouble match, a few of the kids' friends came over. No one left the game board. Their friends had this look on their faces, as if to say, "That's not a video game. It's not even Atari." How could we be so intent on playing such a low-tech game?

Yet the game faces were on.

You know how, in *The Godfather*,'where revenge was called "just business"and was "nothing personal?"

In Trouble, everything is personal. Instead of sending someone to start over from scratch as a last resort, we have been known to plot ways to do this. It is mother against child, sibling vs. sibling warfare, but at least it brings us all around the table as a family. It's heartwarming, really.

So while the kids' friends were over, trying to make sense of it all, the drama began.

One player accused the rest of the table of ganging up on him, which was true but only because he had gone after each of our thimbles on purpose. We knew this because he sang a happy little song about it as he made each of us start over.

We didn't merely gang up on him. We formed a grand alliance against him

When we pointed out to him the treachery of his ways, what prompted us to make getting even our goal, he threw a glass of water, only he missed his target and hit himself.

And no one laughed.

OK, we did laugh. A lot.

That will be another story for the counselor.

STUFF

It's not often I can watch TV and feel good about what our house looks like.

Normally, you would look at whatever was on TV and, even though you knew in your heart of hearts that the Brady Bunch's home was really a set in Hollywood, it made you feel a little deficient. They had six kids, for crying out loud, and no clutter. None. I realize they had the live-in housekeeper, Alice, but one Alice, in real life, cannot keep up with the clutter six kids can produce.

Nothing was ever out of place, covered with fingerprints or spilled.

We can't go 10 minutes without that happening, and there are only four Oeth kids.

But most of all, they didn't have clutter. Of course they didn't. It wasn't real. In real life, children have papers from school. There are magazines and junk mail we might want to keep. Never mind the mail we really do need to keep, such as bills that need paying. There's the great glass migration from the kitchen to every other room in the house. There are clothes here and there in spots other than closets and washing machines.

But mostly, there's stuff. I can watch all kinds of TV shows and they do not have stuff here and there in their pretend homes.

The A&E TV show "Hoarders," though. They have lots of stuff. They have all the stuff that didn't go into those fake TV homes, only their homes are in real life. I realize that hoarding is a serious disorder, and I do not mean to make light of it. But I would be lying if I didn't watch that show and then look around our place and think, "Well, this isn't so bad."

People accumulate stuff. Maybe it goes back to our days as hunter-gatherers. We still hunt and we still gather, and what we hunt and gather now is stuff.

What we have to remember, though, is that people are not their things.

Grandpa, my daddy, had a coffee maker, and every night he would put coffee and water in it, so in the morning, he could click it on and coffee would brew while he dressed. One night, he loaded in the coffee and water and then proceded to have a heart attack. He was never able to drink that pot of coffee.

I couldn't part with it. I couldn't brew the coffee, but I couldn't put the coffee maker away, either.

Years went by before I could wash it and put it in a cabinet, and when I did, I cried and cried. It was an acknowledgement that he wasn't coming back.

Anyone who's had to clean out a family member's home knows how intensely personal that person's things were, and how painful it is to go through them one by one. My mama's penchant for following the British royal family led to a stack of magazines including some from the coronation of Queen Elizabeth II. In that same house were hundreds of gospel LPs, all four-part harmony and tinged with bluegrass, all owned by my daddy. Some of mama's opera albums were there, too.

In our house at one time were lots of drawings, all done by my children. I hailed each one as the best I had ever seen, and each was. Their personalities were captured by the angles of the crayon strokes, the crooked smiles, the family and our pets, one son's love of baseball and another's fascination with monsters.

Those boys are men now, and hanging onto those manila paper sketches won't reverse time any more than keeping a coffee maker ready to brew but never letting it percolate would bring back my daddy.

As much as things can remind us of people, they are not the same thing. Stuff can at times get in the way of people. If you're losing things because you haven't parted with your children's papers from last year, or you won't have friends over because there's too much clutter, then stuff is getting in the way of people, and people do matter more than things.

I've often wondered what archaeologists in the future would think of excavations of our homes. Would they question what we hung onto? What would it tell them about what we valued?

Hanging onto the past, emotionally as well as just having the remnants of what used to be, can keep you from moving ahead. Your arms may be too busy hanging on to stuff from what used to be to grab onto what is and what is to come.

Instead of looking around and thinking things aren't just awful, that, "eh, it could be worse," I should be making room for the wonderful. It's clearing out my children's old things to accommodate who they are now. Creating a space for who each of us are is what we should be about.

It doesn't have to be Brady Bunch perfect. It just has to fit the now, leaving space for the future.

Besides, if I am going to stockpile something, it should be memories. Those take up a lot less space and never need dusting.

HOME IMPROVEMENT

Happiness, it turns out, comes in cans.

Paint cans.

Sometimes life can be overwhelming if you look at it as one big lump. Sometimes it's so big a job that you don't know where to start.

Sometimes that place is a hardware store and the beginning is in the opening of a paint can.

All kinds of things needed fixing up in my world, but one glaring thing was our home. There was and still is a great big ol' list of jobs large and small. It was and still does dwarf time, money and energy.

Trying to get through life was my main objective for more years than I'd like to admit. Getting by. Not thriving, not necessarily joyful. Just surviving.

A hint for those who look at someone's home and wonder why they don't do something about it. The reason might be that as long as the plumbing works and the roof doesn't leak, there are bigger fish to fry in that person's life.

Among my fish, admittedly not the largest one in the cornmeal, was the wallpaper in our home. A very large plaid that at one time was quite fashionable. It was also pink and in the kitchen, so everyone saw it. It was one of the first things you would notice as you walked in.

As one of the Dear Sons once quipped, "How could you not?"

I was once asked if the price of the house was reduced to take the wallpaper into account. It wasn't.

I would watch those shows where people would take a sledgehammer to their kitchen cabinets and counters and scrape all the wallpaper off in an attempt to flip a down-at-the-heels house, and I would dream about a kitchen remodel. I would even figure in my head how much it would cost. I'd visit stores, just to visit the kitchen of my dreams, one without pink plaid wallpaper.

But the wallpaper was still there, and nothing would change.

It's a special person who not only asks to hear about your dreams and repairs, but then rolls up his sleeves and helps you make them. My Gentleman Friend heard me list all the reasons I couldn't part with that wallpaper. He listened to me come up with reason after reason I couldn't make other changes. It all took money, or time, or some sort of a plan, and I didn't have a lot of any of those things.

"A bucket of Kilz isn't that expensive," he said.

We then went to look at paint chips, picking some in yellows and curry and pumpkin and creamy white.

I took the cards out and taped them to the walls, trying to imagine the changes. Figuring I couldn't do worse, I painted over the wallpaper a couple of times. If Kilz can cover kids' crayon murals, it could cover the intersecting green and pink lines of my kitchen walls.

And somehow the challenges I was facing didn't seem quite as large. Then came a warm, spice-colored coat of paint. The dining area was painted a sunny but soft yellow. Every brush stroke did more than improve our home. It improved my view, of the kitchen and of life.

"It's amazing how much joy you got out of a few cans of paint," my Gentleman Friend said.

I stood alone in the middle of the house after he'd gone home, leaving me to admire our work. I marveled over it. The cabinets had a shiny fresh coat of paint, and their knobs were polished until they shone. I didn't want to stop looking.

I still have plenty of things on my list, but doing what we can, when we can, whittles it down a little every day. Making today a better place to live in beats not starting.

ROAD TRIPS

A Civic, four kids and a mom, plus the eqivalent of super-sized fries sprinkled on the floorboard of the back seat.

Picture it in your mind. Smell it. Feel it.

That's a road trip for our family these days. It's a daunting thought, really.

Back when Baby Daddy was around, we'd make car trips from time to time, and he would drive. Always. Because if I drove, who knows when we might get there. I brake for antique shops and Amish quilts, historical markers and Stuckey's with their pecan divinity logs. Once any of those things get involved, time no longer has any meaning to me.

For men, the time it takes to drive somewhere is a direct correlation to their manhood. Keep the schedule, says their inner Ralph Kramden, and yes, he screams that, along with something about someone going to the moon if she mentions the Amish quilts one more time. No stops for a Coke because if you drink, then you have to make a potty stop. Family vacation can turn into the Cannonball Run.

What is it with men and directions?

If I am lost, I pull over to a safe area and ask for help if I can't figure out things with a combination of my iPhone and my son's GPS. But I am a woman.

Men, in contrast, have never been lost because none of them will ever admit to being lost. But if a man ever did say he was lost, he would keep driving. Back in the days before smartphones and Garmins, that was all they could do. You knew they were lost because they would say their meandering path was the "scenic route" and you knew better because (a) you were in a bad neighborhood with windows that were either broken or had burglar bars on them, and (b) Ralph Kramden would never, ever take the scenic route.

Since we now have technology they can check their routes, just for confirmation, but they don't always pull over to do this, because it might appear that they are lost.

The worst thing a kid can ask their daddy on a road trip is, "Are we lost?" The next worst thing is "Are we there yet?"

The worst thing a mama can say on a road trip is, "Why don't we pull over and ask for directions?"

This is true because a man doesn't hear, "Why don't we pull over and ask for directions?" He hears, "Why don't you just hand the keys over, you pansy?"

In their minds, a real man has a built-in GPS that he himself invented before Al Gore got around to inventing the internet. Question his sense of direction and you are questioning his manhood. You might as well tell him to start wearing pink lace-trimmed bloomers.

Years went by before I wanted to dare take a road trip in which I was driving. It's a lot of responsibility. I was picturing us being so lost that we wound up in Canada or Mexico. I was picturing the car with a flat on the side of the interstate with a serial killer volunteering to help change the tire. I was picturing me driving off a cliff or something. Nothing I was picturing was good. I didn't want to shoulder the responsibility of driving because some days just keeping everyone happy and healthy at home with the car parked in the driveway is a challenge.

But the older Dear Sons left the nest, first to college and then to jobs. They're in two different states. So the love of my boys made me a brave single mama, and we decided—I decided—that we were taking a road trip, first to Kansas City, and then to Memphis.

We hit the road, fueling ourselves with road food whenever we stopped to fuel the Civie named Pearl, which is not that often. What she lacks in space, she makes up for in gas stinginess. The teen and the tween slept, awakening for more fried stuff every few hours.

I kept a Diet Coke going. Caffeine is God's gift to single mamas and features editors. I take a sip and thank Jesus.

And mile by mile, I felt more confident. I was fine during the long stretches of interstate. It was hitting cities such as Memphis and St. Louis that scared me. More cars equal more chance of me somehow wrecking Pearl and killing us all.

I prayed through the interchanges, alternately talking about how proud I was of the boys for setting out to seek their fortunes and how amazed I was that they could navigate city traffic. More than once in the city of Memphis I rededicated my life to Christ.

But Pearl was unscathed, and so were we. And I had the perk of stopping wherever and whenever I wanted. I took tee-tee breaks all over the state of Missouri. No one worried about keeping to a schedule because we really didn't have one. Showing up in Kansas City in time to take the oldest Dear Son to dinner was about as much schedule as we had, and city people keep their restaurants open late.

On the way back, there was the field trip to a winery. Who knew that people in Missouri make wine? Turns out, they have wine country there. The only problem was that most of these wineries were off the beaten path. Like 20 miles one way off the interstate.

I had to question whether I wanted to drive an extra forty miles to visit a winery.

The answer was no. But then I found one in Ste. Genevieve that was a mere five miles from the exit. Turns out, I might not want to drive forty miles for wine, but it has been proven that I will drive a 10-mile round trip for a bottle or three.

So with the youngest Dear Son snoring in the back seat, the Dear Daughter and I headed into the little farming town of Ste. Genevieve. Turns out they have some awesome art galleries there, too, along with a winery at the end of a path marked by signs painted with bunches of grapes.

If we had a schedule, it was blown. But that is the beauty of not having a schedule. You can't blow to smithereens what you never had in the first place. We looked at paintings, strolled a little and by the time we turned around to get back on the interstate, there was a bottle of white, a bottle of red and a bottle of pink wine in the car.

You can call it rose' if you want. It was pink. And, it turns out, delicious with a little cheese and some mutligrain crackers, the kind that make you feel healthier than thou just for eating them. It was a nice carrot at the end of the stick, thinking about a nice glass of wine once I got home. Don't judge.

We also stopped, just outside of Memphis, at the Dixie Queen. They have a ridiculous number of flavors of soft-serve ice cream. Totally worth blowing a non-existent schedule. I got an enormous pina colada-flavored ice cream cone and a brain freeze. Totally worth it.

We did have one mishap, or actually our cat did. She managed to shut herself into a room, forgetting that she doesn't have thumbs and couldn't reach the doorknobs if she had them. The Gentleman Friend rescued her.

Before long, we had pulled in the driveway and the washing machine was going. We had all kinds of memories, from watching the Royals and eating barbecue in Kansas City to watching the ducks at the Peabody in Memphis, not to mention getting the whole family together again.

It was well worth a few tanks of gas and a little white-knuckle driving. I'm already planning the next road trip.

Part 5

Matters of the Heart

The meeting was, if not impossible, improbable.

Shirley was a single elementary teacher in her mid 30s. Her friend Carole, also a teacher, wanted to go to California on vacation in the summer of 1959. Shirley didn't want to go. She had just been there in 1958, and vacation money wasn't plentiful for teachers, not now and especially not then in Oklahoma, where they lived.

"Well, if you won't go, then I'll just stay home," Carole said.

Then it would be Shirley's fault that her best friend sat home in Oklahoma City instead of going on vacation. It was going to California with her best friend or going on a guilt trip. California it was, on a Greyhound bus that would stop for visits to tourist meccas and homes of the stars.

Taylor, about 30 at the time, wasn't planning to go to California, either. He had another trip picked out, but it wasn't available. He couldn't get a refund, but he was offered the trip out west. He wasn't thrilled, but he also wanted a vacation from the family trucking business in Mississippi, so California it was.

That's how Shirley and Taylor wound up on the same bus.

Nobody remembered who spoke to whom first.

Shirley said she smiled at Taylor and told Carole she thought he was nice-looking. Taylor noticed her at Carlsbad Caverns. She was pretty, he'd recall.

Shirley wore a yellow dress and high heels that hurt her feet.

"She still walked real fast," he said, remembering keeping a brisk pace to keep up with her in those stilettos.

Somewhere in those caverns, they struck up a friendship. During their time away from the Greyhound, they caught a movie, strolled, shared dinners and talked. About everything. And nothing.

"She was the one," he'd say.

When Taylor and Shirley parted company, they wrote letter after letter to each other in those pre-internet, pre-email days. A letter a day. Phone calls weren't cheap, and in West Point, Mississippi, in 1959, they weren't necessarily private. Operators not only were needed to call someone, but they might ask why you wanted to talk to them. But Taylor would call her every weekend.

He even caught a flight or two in Memphis to visit Shirley and her parents. The third time he went to Oklahoma City, it was to get married.

The families had their reservations. "You barely know each other," Taylor and Shirley heard over and over again.

"You're just going to quit your job and get married and move to Mississippi?" Shirley's older brother argued.

Taylor's family wondered if she was a gold digger. They needn't have worried.

Both said that first year took some getting used to. The family home, where Taylor grew up, still lived and would call home until retirement, had been in need of a woman's touch, and both had lived on their own long enough to make moving in a little bumpy.

Once she packed her car, the bare-basics Ford she bought with cash saved from teaching and working part-time at an amusement park, but Taylor asked her not to go. The suitcases went back into the house.

Before long, the rollercoaster of distance romance love letters and getting used to married life smoothed out into a loving partnership. Her diary entries were about putting the finishing touches on a dress she was sewing or about the two going off to gospel singings. Never mind that Shirley was an opera fan before she married. Taylor loved hymns like "Have A Little Talk With Jesus" and four-part harmony, so she took up going to singings.

Taylor worked hard, getting up before dawn and working past dark, and Shirley made home a haven.

Born with bad eyes, Taylor never had sight good enough for driving a car, and Shirley worried over him riding his Cushman scooter around town. She drove Taylor wherever he wanted to go, and later, when rheumatoid arthritis would cripple her painfully and slowly, Taylor would be her legs. He would walk here and there, running errands.

As her health failed, he began cleaning. Laundry was a particular point of pride for him, and the man who rarely ever fixed his own plate since saying "I do" was cooking for them both when standing became more difficult.

Try as he might, her care became overwhelming for him, and her doctor recommended moving into a nursing home. Taylor spent each day with her, talking on the porch for hours, him in a rocker and Shirley in a wheelchair. They were just like that younger couple in California, passengers on the journey of life, taking it all in, chatting, people watching and holding hands.

One day, Shirley, always a pretty sharp tack, didn't make sense. "Your mama is talking, but I don't understand her," he said.

Just like Taylor's mother many years before, Shirley was having a stroke, the first of several. A later one would leave her unable to communicate and bedridden. Taylor still spent each day with her, holding her hand and talking to her, hoping she'd open her eyes and say his name.

Shirley never did.

Taylor was with her when she died, not wanting to believe that for the first time in 44 years, he'd be without her.

Teetotalers, they never shared a glass of champagne, and both would rather have dined on burgers at a well-lit diner than on things they couldn't pronounce at a candlelight dinner. But romances don't get any better than the love Taylor and Shirley shared.

They're both gone now, Taylor just a couple of years after Shirley. The love of my mama and daddy, I like to think, lives on.

THE WIDOW CARD

This always takes some explaining.

I am the mother of four, which usually has someone asking if it is a blended family. It's not. All my babies can claim me and Baby Daddy as their mama and daddy.

If I tell people the truth, that I am a widow with four children, it is a buzz kill. Their day is ruined. It's like people think I am just now discovering, by listening to my own words, that I'm a widow and that they, by asking about Baby Daddy, had somehow brought all this about.

I went through this so much at a class reunion that the next time a classmate said, "Where's that husband of yours?" I was going to reply, "He couldn't be here tonight," which would have been true.

But if I tell someone I am a single mother with four children, you know some immediately begin to pass judgement. Before you know it, someone is thinking I have four different baby daddies and no wedding band. Or four wedding bands. Or I'm making a living off collecting child support. Who knows? But I know the looks I have gotten when saying I am a single mother with four children, and they weren't as sympathetic as the widow looks.

I can either go the route of playing the widow card or being who knows what to total strangers.

By the way, I can tell you from my brief time on Match.com, that telling some men you are a widow with four children can make them run a four-minute mile. Usually this was done via email, so I didn't see the actual cloud of dust kicked up by them running away, but I could visualize it. It was a big cloud of dust, just like in the Road Runner cartoons. I liked to imagine the cartoon sound effects to go with it.

Really, playing the widow card was a nice test. It sent the riff-raff packing. Quickly.

There are perks of being a bereaved spouse. One is the casseroles. I didn't feel like eating, but still, people were sweet to me and brought us casseroles. I didn't have to cook for a month, and I had two teenagers and two young children home at the time. Might as well be a swarm of locusts, as those kids like to eat. Divorced moms and single moms don't get as many casserole gifts.

Another is a stunt the second Dear Son did when taking his driver's license test. When his driver's text examiner was waffling on whether to pass him or not, the Dear Son, who really should have been accompanied by violin music, proceeded to tell his tale.

"My mother's a widow, sir, and she works so hard every day," he began. "I just need my license so I can drive from my high school to the community college, where I will be taking classes this fall. If I could drive there, it would make her life just a little bit easier."

All of this was true, by the way, but the second Dear Son has a flair for telling the truth with maximum dramatic effect. Listening to him tell it, I was all but scrubbing floors into the wee hours of the morning Cinderella-style.

"Ma'am, is this true?" the examiner asked.

"Yes," I said, "And he will only be driving to and from school"

This was also true because his car was what is known as a hooptie. A beater. A jalopy. He might have been driving to and from school in it, but it wasn't going to be at anything over 45 miles per hour.

No tales were told, and the license was gotten.

But there are some huge downsides. Being the Lone Ranger is one of them. As a friend and fellow widow told me, "I know that I don't have anyone to blame things on but myself." You laugh, married people, but even if you don't outright blame each other, at least you aren't making bad decisions alone.

There is also missing the one other person on the planet who loved our children as much as I did. Half the parenting team was gone.

Then there is grief, in all its five stages. I think I made a round trip through all of them before hitting Acceptanceville. Denial is the best stop. A swim in Denial River beats anger and depression by a mile. I still try to vacation in Denial every so often.

Widowhood is not something I would have chosen for myself, but it got dealt into my hand anyway. Looking back on the eight years or so since I became one, I can say it's changed my life and changed who I am. I choose to look at only the good outcomes and not dwell on stones in the road getting there. Some days I have to will myself, force myself, not to dwell there. Nobody ever said it would be easy.

Being a widow made me brave, though.

It is like being a mama bear on steroids. If I was a devoted mother before, I had to become twice that just to keep up.

It has made me more understanding, less likely to judge, more likely to realize that we're all just trying to get through our days and that if we're getting through them, we might as well find as much joy along the way as possible.

Being a widow made me realize that our time here is a fleeting thing, so no "I love yous" should go unsaid. Those you love should know they're loved. You should never miss out on time with friends and family. You can't waste a day or even a moment.

When you get handed something like a widow card in your life, God makes sure you wind up stronger for the experience of that card being played. You wind up doing things you would have never dreamed you could do and thinking thoughts you never would have thought otherwise.

You just play the hand you're dealt the best way you know how.

MY FAVORITE TV SHOW

College is a new "episode" for parents and students. It's like you've been watching your favorite TV show for eighteen years, I remember Joe Paul saying.

201

You love the main character. You laugh at his jokes. You're his biggest fan. You know what he ate for breakfast and what he wore and when he's coming home and who his friends are.

You watch this show every single day. And then all of a sudden, your show's not on. You might have to wait weeks to see it again, or until a holiday special comes on.

This is what it's like when your child goes away to college, said Paul, vice president of student affairs at the University of Southern Mississippi, to us first-time college parents at an orientation program.

Now not only do you not know what your favorite character ate for breakfast, you don't know if he ate breakfast, or whether he woke up on time, if he had a pen with him in class or whether he made friends on campus. And who are these new friends, anyway?

I have had to stop watching "my favorite TV shows" twice so far, and I can tell you, it is not easy giving them up.

I knew my boys were going to good schools, and I had such great memories of my own college years that I wanted them to grow and find themselves just as I had. Our goal as a family is a college degree for each child, so this was a dream coming to fruition. It was a happy and exciting time, yet a difficult and bittersweet one.

Sending my oldest off to Southern Miss was, at first, fun. I spent the summer before shopping for dorm gear, learning about USM and making sure we did lots of fun things together as a family. I was in denial that my show was not going to be on each day, right up until we finished moving everything into the dorm.

Then the dam burst, and the tears began to flow.

"Mom, you're going to see me in a couple of weeks. Mom, it's going to be OK. Mom, I'll call you every day, I promise.''

No matter what my son said, I just kept on boo-hooing. Because I love that TV show, and I was really going to miss it.

Eventually, I pulled myself together for the drive back home and stopped off at the Watermelon Patch, a Hattiesburg mecca for shoes and ice cream. I browsed around and thought I was going to be fine.

Then I get in the car, pull out of the parking lot, and next on the mix CD in the car stereo was Little Big Town. Singing "Stay.'' And staaaaaay just a little bit longer, 'til I'm a little bit stronger to take all this. And staaaaaay just a little more time 'til I can find a way. Please stay . . .

Curse you, Little Big Town, I lost it again.

All the way from Collins to Ridgeland, I sobbed. I got home and took the younger sibs to Bright Lights, Belhaven Nights, thinking it would cheer me up. But I thought all weekend long about the missing piece to our family puzzle and whether he was lost or hungry.

Little by little, though, it got easier. I didn't blow up his cell phone the next week, and I refused to be a helicopter mom, hovering over my grown son. He was a man, and I was going to treat him like one.

Our family went back to Hattiesburg a few weeks later for a home game tailgate, and not only did my favorite TV show have a cool new setting, the main character looked great. He knew his way around campus, had plenty of friends and looked healthy and happy. His clothes were clean because he washed them, not me.

He was obviously loving class and talked about all the subjects he was studying. I was liking this new story line, even if I didn't get to watch every single day.

Oh, that show? It's still on. The main character graduated from USM in 2011. The commencement episode was awesome.

--Reprinted from The Clarion-Ledger

SPENDING TIME

Time management is a popular topic these days. You can cruise through any business section of any book store and find shelves of titles on this topic.

I like to read such titles. I figure if I only get 24 hours in a day I should manage them better than I manage my checking account. There's no such thing as a time overdraft. Plus, reading these in the company breakroom makes me look like I am at least trying. Some days, I may be holding up one of those business books, but there's really a *People* magazine inside. But I look like I'm a management genius.

On one of the days I was reading a business book and not *People*, the author asked the rhetorical question of what a company's greatest asset was. People, is what he said most business leaders would say. And that's a popular answer, but a wrong one.

Time, he wrote. That's a company's greatest asset. More people can be hired, but you can't get more time. Tempus is always fugiting. "Like sands through the hour glass,'' I remember hearing on TV when my mama would watch her stories, "so are the Days of our Lives." And that sand slows down for no one.

Time's more important than money. There's a saying that if your problem can be fixed with money, then it's not a real problem. That's true for everything but real money problems, because money can fix those right up.

There's also the saying about "buying time.'' We'll buy time by making a small repair and hoping the car doesn't blow up.

But you can't really buy time. If we could, it would be out of our price range. Or I'd get some humdrum old piece of time, spent being bored, or worse, maybe time spent getting a root canal or having the flu.

Good time, though. That stuff is priceless.

I take this time management stuff pretty seriously. To the point that I listen to CDs of books when I commute some days. On one of those CDs, the author recommended thinking about what we do each day and asking whether it was enjoyable and whether it was beneficial.

If you think about it, it will amaze and horrify you how much time we spend on things we don't enjoy and are not beneficial. Email, for instance. I was happy to hear that the Department of Homeland Security was reading my email. I would happily delegate that task to them. It's not the most enjoyable thing in the world to do, but sometimes it is beneficial. Some Nigerian prince was emailing me just the other day about giving me $1 million if he could just park some money in my bank account. All he needed was an account number.

Yeah, I know. It's not beneficial all the time, and the Nigerian prince is never beneficial.

How much mindless TV do we watch? Exercise is always beneficial, but how much do you enjoy it? Eating isn't always enjoyable, and it isn't always beneficial. I have gone mindless, eating stale tater chips while watching something stupid on TV just because I was too lazy to change the channel or find something better in the kitchen.

I used to think that time management was about getting stuff done. More stuff crammed into the same 24 hours.

It's not that, although nobody can cram stuff into a day like a mama can. Picture an overstuffed suitcase, and we mamas are jumping up and down on it, trying to pack just one more thing in.

Doing more things isn't the answer. Doing the right things, things that are fun and beneficial, is. You put that test to what you do, and what's a waste of time suddenly isn't. Things that you think are productive aren't. It might change your mind about what you do and what you delegate.

Conversation is never wasted time. Southerners know this from back when there wasn't air conditioning and sitting on the porch talking was a way to keep cool. When you're talking, you're developing a relationship.

I could have delegated driving my younger children to one of their brothers, but then I would have missed talking to them when they're a captive audience. Now they ride the bus and get that same talking time with their friends, which is what they need in those teen and tween years.

Time petting a purring kitten is never wasted.

Eating ice cream is never a waste of time. It's enjoyable, and while it may not benefit the waistline, it compensates by benefitting the soul.

Playing fetch with a dog is never wasted time. Ever.

Watching *Sherlock* or *Doctor Who* with your Dear Daughter and her fan girl friends just so you can be with them when they ooh and ahh over Benedict Cumberbatch or discuss the cuteness of the various Doctors is not a waste of time, although it might feel like it at times.

Watching your Dear Sons play "Super Smash Bros.'' is not a waste of time even when you don't know what is going on. Why? Because you get to watch male bonding in action. For you people with no sons, it is like watching the movie *Gorillas in the Mist*. Complete with the screaming. But they love it, you love them, so it's enjoyable and it's time invested in a relationship, so it's beneficial.

Working late? Not enjoyable, and if it leads to neither extra pay or a promotion and keeps you away from precious time with those you love, then it is not beneficial. Keep it to a bare minimum at the worst and zero at the best.

Sitting with your coffee in the still early morning hours while counting your blessings? Never a waste.

Dancing to embarrass your children? Time well spent.

Cleaning the house? A necessary evil.

You want to keep the love at a maximum, laughter high, boredom low to nonexistent. What if we started measuring our time by the amount of good memories we crammed into 24 little hours instead of how much we could get done and how many things we could scratch off our lists?

GROWING OLDER

You live a good life. You work hard, play by the rules, pay your bills, and what do you get?

Your body can betray you. Or your mind does.

Either way, you might not be able to do things you once took for granted. Your children have to exchange roles with you, and the people you once kept from running with scissors and playing in traffic are now trying to take control, telling you you can't drive anymore or that you need help in the everyday and the ordinary. The things you once took for granted.

My Mama and I had to exchange roles. Neither one of us wanted to, but the passing of time and the physical letdowns our bodies hand us as we get older had other ideas.

I moved to the city, some three hours away, at her urging, to follow a career and make a better life for us, but that meant I wasn't there as she got older. Maybe, in hindsight, it helped me see more clearly that she needed help.

I'd come home to visit, and each time, she'd have more medical problems and orders from a home health nurse she would ignore whenever going salt-free was one of the rules.

My daddy would look more tired and would sometimes get confused. Usually happy, he became downcast.

I began to cook for them when I came home instead of the other way around.

After lunch, we'd watch old movies or family videos, they'd doze off and I would watch them. Each time I saw them, they looked older and more tired.

One day, I brought up the idea of retirement living. They wanted nothing to do with it. But then one day, my mama fell down and my daddy wasn't strong enough to pick her up.

I was three hours away trying to comfort a baby and get children to school when I heard them crying on the phone.

She was taken to the hospital by ambulance. Congestive heart failure left her legs swollen, and arthritis had left them gnarled and unsteady. What mobility and balance she had left was quickly leaving. Her doctor told me she needed nursing home care and told me what I already know. As an only child, I was the only one who could handle the situation.

My daddy was nothing but angry, at life in general and me in particular. To him at the time, I was taking his wife away. I don't blame him, because I'd be angry, too. At everything and everyone.

None of it was fair. For anyone.

But our definition of fair isn't what always happens in life.

Looking back, I don't see how any of us handled the situation without losing our minds. My mama was losing her independence and what was left of her health. My daddy was having to admit they needed help, and needing help wasn't something he liked admitting. It may have been a first. I had small children and an even smaller bank account. Nothing was easy for any of us.

But we stuck together. I got time off from work to care for mama in my own home until I could get her the care she needed in a place she came to love. My daddy didn't stay angry forever. He came to visit two weeks later and never came back to their home except to get the rest of his things.

Mama's health improved, and so did Daddy's, since he was no longer carrying around the stress of being an aging caregiver and was living with us, taking away the stress of cooking and running errands.

Mama and Daddy spent their last four years together, seeing each other daily without the hassles of keeping a house and yard up and stretching disability checks as far as they would go.

And me?

If I said it was easy, we'd both know I was lying. My own family was at varying times, incredibly understanding and the polar opposite of that only on steroids. Baby Daddy hadn't signed on for this, he'd say, and he was right. Yet all I could do was make the best of a situation that was difficult for everyone. Multiple times I was told to choose between my marriage and my parents, something no one should be told to do.

But there are blessings for those of us who care or have cared for aging parents. One is that you have three, or sometimes four, generations interacting. Having grandparents or great-grandparents to talk with is a treasure, even if it comes in the disguise of a situation no one wants.

You can know that you are making family a priority. For us, it was a time for children to know their roots and for their grandparents to take pride in their babies' babies. And they did. The boys were always a joy to their Grandma whenever we all got together, and the Dear Daughter? All she had to do was smile, and both Grandma and Grandpa were wrapped around her finger. This happened often. The girl could do no wrong.

Those in the sandwich generation, between young children and aging parents, also know that they are honoring their parents by making the best decisions they can for them. At first, getting my parents the care they needed seemed like something that only brought them frustration with life, but later they both thanked me.

I learned that being there for my parents as they grew older was a blessing because I could, in a small way, return the favor for the many times they were there for me.

But ultimately, caring for aging parents is not something you do to return favors. It has nothing to do with who they are. Instead, it is about who you are.

Life may not always be fair. It has stones in the road and potholes. The best we can do is to help those we love in slowly walking around the rough patches.

MATTERS OF THE HEART

To many people, hearts are what you draw around the name of your beloved in the margins of notebooks. They are lined with lace and flowers on Valentine's Day, frilly things made of paper.

While they're pretty and conjure up sweet thoughts, they're not real hearts. Real hearts can be broken. Sometimes real hearts can be mended, and sometimes not.

My oldest son was born with a broken heart.

He wasn't pink like most babies gulping down oxygen. His skin was darker, and his breathing seemed to take a lot of effort. After days of tests and a flight to the University of Mississippi Medical center, the broken part of his heart was a pulmonary vein that was not connected to the rest of his heart.

The body's will to live being an incredible thing, this baby less than a week old was rerouting his blood to bypass the area that needed mending. It was enough to keep him alive, but not enough for him to live very long.

He would need surgery on an area smaller than my thumbnail. After hours of painstaking work, the mend was made. The boy, a 9-pound, 11-ounce baby who dwarfed the others in the NICU, had turned pink, loads of oxygen flooding his body for the first time since his birth. He was beautiful, even though he was mostly bandages and tubes.

He wasn't through scaring us yet, hemorrhaging once and then having fluid build up on his lungs. He also liked to take his IVs out and wasn't used to being held when being poked or proded wasn't involved.

Still, his mended heart kept beating. Pretty soon, he was not only alive but thriving, a little boy intent on catching frogs, climbing trees and riding his bicycle farther than allowed. He grew into a teenager and was getting ready for his high school graduation.

Baby Daddy's heart was always filled with dreams for his children, but his heart became broken, too, the year we would have been celebrating the oldest boy's 18th birthday.

One Sunday afternoon, Baby Daddy went from grilling outside to chest pains that he passed off as nothing. They weren't.

Though he argued with everyone in the house about dialing 911, help was called, prompting bouts of hollering between chest pains. He left with the ambulance crew, his heart attack taking his life before he got to a hospital.

I had no idea.

I left the children watching each other and went from hospital to hospital, trying to find Baby Daddy. Still smarting from the argument over 911, I was thinking of all the "I told you sos" I could give him. I thought about how he was going to have to eat a healthy diet and give up smoking. More "I told you sos."

It never occurred to me he'd go away forever. There were a lot of things that should have been said that weren't.

Before he left the house, Dear Daughter, four at the time, picked dandelions for her daddy and drew him a collection of hearts because she loved him and she was young enough to believe that a crayoned heart could heal a real one.

I proceeded to spend hours at University Medical Center trying to make sense of what didn't, losing my car in the parking lot and wondering how on earth I was going to raise four children as a widow.

But life went on. Because that is what life does.

About five months later, my father, known around our house as Grandpa, couldn't get comfortable. Grandpa was a part of our family, and we all lived in the same house.

"My arm hurts," he said after supper one summer evening.

"Are you also having chest pains, shortness of breath?" I asked, running down whatever heart attack symptoms came to mind.

"No, it's just Arthur," he laughed. "Arthur" was short for "Arthur Itis," a joke of his about the pains of growing older.

"Arthur Itis has a brother named Burse," he'd joke.

Grandpa took a Tylenol and went off to bed.

An hour later, he came out of his bedroom.

"My arm still hurts," he said.

911 got a call.

"If I'd have known you were going to call them, I'd have kept this to myself," Grandpa said.

He wound up with a two-week hospital stay punctuated with heart attacks and failed stents. A stent would hold open a blocked area for a day or two, then fail, and the chest pains would begin. Each time this happened, Grandpa and his heart grew weaker.

After one particularly hard day, Grandpa looked me in the eye and said, "I love you, but you have to let me go. If it is my time, let me go."

"Dad, it's just been a hard day. Tomorrow will be better."

For him it was. He got to wake up seeing Jesus. His old heart was of no use to him anymore.

Hearts can be incredibly strong, yet incredibly fragile. They can take the strain of living until one day they don't. They beat and beat and beat until one day they can't.

They are a symbol of our life force, our souls.

"Put your heart into it."

"He's got a lot of heart."

Matters of the heart are those held close, that can bring happiness, like the thriving of a child who almost died but is now a grown man, or grief, when a loved one leaves our lives. Whether it is a life saved through the mending of a heart or a life lost because there were no heartbeats left, our days must be lived with heart.

Never miss an opportunity to reveal your heart, to give from the heart, and to love with your whole heart.

GIRLFRIENDS

Little girls have best friends.

They play Barbies together, do each other's hair and make cootie catchers, those little folded pieces of paper that have numbers and colors on them. Depending on the numbers and colors we picked, one of us could have married Shaun Cassidy, the Justin Bieber of his day. We'd look for four-leafed clovers and talk about boys.

Later on, though, our female friends take a back seat. We go to college and get serious about our careers or our boyfriends or both. We have babies, and all these become our world.

This is a sad thing, because careers come and go. There's news items every day about downsizings and reductions in force, a nice way of saying "layoffs" without sugarcoating it to the point of calling them "rightsizings." When I was graduating from Mississippi University for Women, the scent of flowers from the Magnolia Chain still on my hands, I remember the speaker saying that, on their death beds, no one ever wished for more time at the office. Although more time at the office would beat out being on a death bed, a better alternative would be anywhere else. Even if you love your job, it's not going to last. The lucky retire, but to what?

Marriages and relationships don't last forever. The good boyfriends stay and might become husbands, and the others go. Notice the jewelry ads said "Diamonds are forever.'' The rock has 50-50 odds of outlasting each marriage, and that doesn't take into account what happened to me, becoming a widow at forty.

And mamas, you may either cheer or boo-hoo over this, but your children will not be here forever. They grow up. I have lived through two of them moving out and off to other states, and you know what? The other two will probably do the same thing. They will have their own homes and friends and jobs that won't have a thing in the world to do with me.

But your girlfriends? They are forever.

They won't make cootie catchers with you anymore, but they'll take you off on a girls' trip to Pigeon Forge after your husband dies.

The four of us lived in three different states, and life . . . jobs, husbands, children and budgets . . . meant that we went years without seeing each other.

We weren't just alike anymore. Some of us got up early, some slept in until 10 and some had to be dragged out of bed at noon. One of us wanted to ride horseback through Cade's Cove, one wanted to hit whatever rollercoasters Dollywood had to offer, and the other two said, "No, thanks.'' There were only about four patches of common ground on that trip: Eating pancakes, drinking margaritas, shopping at the outlets and talking just like we used to.

We did all four really well, especially the last one. It was like I'm-not-gonna-say-how-many years hadn't passed. We were sitting up late talking about anything or nothing. Girlfriends stick around, even when they're not around all the time.

Your girlfriends are the ones who, just like they did when you get your heart broken in junior high only you are now in your forties, remind you that the guy who stomped on your feelings wasn't worth having. They never liked him anyway, they'll tell you.

They'll also affirm you. Want to feel skinny while you are eating white chocolate bread pudding? Go out for dessert with your girlfriends. On these outings, we splurge on dessert and tell each other we can afford it because of how slim we are.

We also tell each other we're smart and funny and gorgeous, and we never lie.

If a girlfriend of ours gets a number from what I will call a Man Not Worth Having, we wad it up and throw it away if burning it is not an option. A pre-emptive strike. Lord only knows how many numbers we wish we'd have wadded up for friends, but hindsight is 20/20.

Your girlfriends will go walking with you for miles and miles. We get to talking and before we know it, we've gone five miles, so that means we have to turn around and walk five miles back because that's where our cars are.

They run with you and tell you that you don't smell bad, even when you stink worse than your teenage son after football practice.

We ooh and ahh over men together, but not in the way you might think. We brag on how one of our fellows fixed a pipe or repaired a gate without being asked, or just showed up with flowers or wanted to know, when he found out his sweetie was having a bad day, what he could do to make it better. Those, by the way, we're going to call Men Worth Having.

We remind each other of this. We're a cheering section for the Men Worth Having and are the worst enemies of the other sort.

Why? Well, other than not wanting to see friends with Men Not Worth Having, we know that when they get their hearts hurt, we're going to be the ones hunting for shards of heart that we're going to have to tape together and mend over wine and calories. Wine and calories are fun, but only when you're happy.

The best reason to make time for having girlfriends is that they make you a happier person. Those you love who will miss you while you're getting your time in with your BFFs, but they'll get a smiling and recharged wife, girlfriend or mama in return. And who doesn't want one of those?

You may grow out of your cootie catchers and Barbies, but you never outgrow your girlfriends.

Acknowledgements

I've been blessed with friends far better than I deserve and, expecting love and laughter out of life, I have found more of both than I could imagine. I would like to thank the following people for their awesomeness and encouragement throughout the creative process:

James L. Dickerson, for taking a chance on an idea and being the kind of editor every writer should have.

Leslie Hurst and Brian Tolley, for professional coaching and taking a chance on me more than once.

Joe Lee and Rick Guy, for encouragement and accountability from one writer to another.

Melanie Thortis, for being a patient friend and creative photographer.

My children, who make me believe, in them, myself, God and tomorrows.

Grant Phillips, for listening to my dreams, giving me hope, showing me kindness, and always asking me, "What's next?"

ABOUT THE AUTHOR

A small-town Mississippi girl grows up, snatches a magnolia during her college graduation, and sets out to be a writer, newspaper editor and mama. Annie Oeth has done all three—and lived to tell the tale.

A native of West Point, Mississippi, Oeth began writing from her front porch swing when she wasn't climbing trees and drawing. She is a graduate of Mississippi University for Women, embarking on a journalism career and motherhood soon after. She's written for magazines including *Today's Christian Woman* and newspapers such as *The Commercial Appeal* and *The Commercial Dispatch* in Columbus, Miss.

In 1996, she moved from Mississippi's smallest daily newspaper, *The Daily Times Leader* in West Point, to the state's largest, *The Clarion-Ledger*, in Jackson. Starting as an assistant metro editor, Oeth moved to editing a family of nondaily publications before returning to the daily product as features editor in 2012. She's been writing about family and fun for *The Clarion-Ledger* and in The Mom Zone blog ever since.

Family is the center of her life, and she enjoys watching the lives of her four children unfold. Like her page on Facebook and follow her on Twitter at @Annie0. She lives at Ridgeland, Mississippi.

ABOUT THE PUBLISHER

SARTORIS
LITERARY
GROUP

Sartoris Literary Group, Inc. is a Jackson, Mississippi publisher that is dedicated to telling the stories of the South, both fiction and nonfiction. A traditional publisher, SLG publishes 20-25 titles a year. It is one of the largest online publishers in the South and one of the few publishers in the South that accepts fiction. Unlike five of the seven largest New York publishers, which are all foreign owned, SLG is proudly American owned.

Other Sartoris Literary Group books you may enjoy:

Thursday Morning Breakfast (and Murder) Club
By Liz Stauffer

Wiggle Room
By Darden North

One More Mountain: Road Warriors Explore America
By Janet Buckwalter

Sons Without Fathers: What Every Mother Needs to Know
By Mardi Allen and James L. Dickerson

www.ingramcontent.com/pod-product-compliance
Lightning Source LLC
LaVergne TN
LVHW091216080426
835509LV00009B/1018